MICK WALKER'S
ITALIAN CLASSIC GALLERY

THE RACING BIKES

a **Foulis** Motor Cycling Book

First published 1991

Published by:
Haynes Publishing Group
Sparkford, Nr Yeovil
Somerset BA22 7JJ, England

Haynes Publications Inc
861 Lawrence Drive, Newbury Park,
California 91320, USA

British Library Cataloguing in Publication Data

Walker, Mick
    Classic Italian Racing Motorcycles
    1. Racing motorcycles, history
    I. Title
    629.227

    ISBN 0-85429-835-5

Library of Congress Catalog Card Number
90-84489

Editor: Robin Read
Design: Mike King
Layout: Jill Moulton
Typeset in Times Roman Medium 11/12pt and
printed in England by J. H. Haynes & Co. Ltd

Contents

Acknowledgements

Having been involved with Italian motorcycles for some three decades, and fortunate enough to have ridden, raced, sold, serviced and tuned them, and acted as the British importer for several of the best-known marques, it gives me great pleasure to be able to share with the reader this selection of photographs. The great majority of them come from my own files and have been collected over many years.

I would also like to express my thanks to the following for their help in providing photographs: Placido Gullotta (Aprilia); Norm Westermann and Guido Rinalli (Benelli); Luigi Giacometti (Cagiva); Nadia Pavignani and Franco Valentini (Ducati); Roberto Patrigani (Garelli); Guido Miraglia (Gilera); Tim Parker, Tim Isles, and Richard Slater (Laverda); Peter Glover (Morini); Gemma Pedretta (Moto Guzzi); Signora Ostini, David Kay, Alan Cathcart and Arturo Magni (MV Agusta); Ray Pearce (Rumi); Douglas Jackson (The World's Motorcycle News Agency); the late Count Corrado Agusta; the late Maurice Cann; Brian Clark; Ken Kavanagh; Alan Kirk; Ing. Alfio Morone; Nick Nicholls; Ing. Fabio Taglioni; Tarquinio Provini; Ron Titenor; Philip Tooth; and Steve Wynne.

I would like to record my sincere appreciation of the work of my old friend Robin Read, who has edited this book and its road bike companion.

It now only remains for me to wish you, the reader, as much enjoyment in reading and viewing the contents of the book as I have had in putting it together.

Mick Walker
Wisbech, Cambridgeshire

SETTING THE SCENE

Early Days

For many years Italy lagged behind a number of the other major European countries in the early development of the internal combustion engine, and in particular in the racing activities connected with it. It was France and Britain who led the way, both in the development of suitable machines and in the organization of competitive events. However, Italy did have the satisfaction of at least providing some of the riders.

It was not until after the end of the First World War that the first Italian racing motorcycles began to appear, such as the Garelli two-stroke split single, and four-strokes from Moto Guzzi and Bianchi.

An important day in the history of Italian road racing came on 7 September 1924, when the very first official European Championship meeting was staged at the Monza Autodrome, near Milan. This was limited to the 500 cc category and victory went to Guido Mentasi on a four-valve, horizontal, overhead camshaft Guzzi single.

Until that time it had been the British who had dominated the European – and therefore the world – racing scene. However, throughout the remainder of the 1920s and into the 1930s, a fierce battle for supremacy was waged between the Italians and the British, the Germans also coming into the picture on occasion.

This Anglo-Italian rivalry reached a peak in 1935 when the Irish rider Stanley Woods won both the Lightweight (250 cc) and Senior (500 cc) Tourist Trophies, run over the famous 60.75 km (37.75 mile) Mountain circuit in the Isle of Man. Mounted on works Guzzis – a single and V-twin respectively – Woods made history by becoming the first rider to score a double on motorcycles not manufactured in Britain.

This success in what was at that time, and for many years afterwards the world's premier road racing event, gave not only Moto Guzzi, but Italian bikes in general, an emphatic credibility.

The first TT had been staged back in 1907. Its fame had led others to copy it, and by the early 1920s Italy had three similar events: the Targa Florio, the Savio circuit and the Lario event.

The last of these was arguably the most famous, being/ run over a 50 km (31 mile) circuit on mountain roads near the Guzzi factory, at Mandello del Lario on the shores of Lake Como, in northern Italy.

The *Circuito del Lario,* to give the event its Italian title, began in 1921 (a year after the local Moto Guzzi marque started up in business) and was the nearest the Italians came to a replica of the Isle of Man course. It was held annually thereafter until the outbreak of the Second World War, except for two interruptions in the early 1930s brought about by the Depression. Star rider in the series was the legendary Tazio Nuvolari, who won the 350 cc category four years running on his factory Bianchi double-knocker single.

Another famous Bianchi rider of the era was Achille Varzi (who also rode Guzzis). Like Nuvolari, Varzi won equal fame on two and four wheels. This versatility was quite a feature of the Italian racing scene in the inter-war years: Gilera's Piero Taruffi was another master of both crafts.

The 1930s witnessed some truly great victories not only for Bianchi and Guzzi, but also for the Gilera company. This concern gained greatly from taking over the development of the Rondine ('Swallow') four-cylinder racer, conceived first by OPRA, and carried on by CNA.

The Rondine had its origins in 1923 when two young engineers, Carlo Gianini and Piero Remor, who had just graduated from Rome University, sat down to map out a high-performance motorcycle engine. A feature of their creation was the idea of setting the four cylinders across the frame, and so solving at a stroke the problems of cooling and drive that had plagued the earlier inline types.

The OPRA-CNA-Gilera configuration was a truly innovative piece of engineering; it was to set the standard for the future post-war era not just in Italy, but around the world. Besides Gilera, MV Agusta, Benelli and the Japanese Honda company were all to employ a similar layout with great success.

In 1937 the Guzzi rider Omobono Tenni became the first Italian on an Italian machine to win in the Isle of Man, when he came first in the Lightweight TT. By 1939, the Italian challenge for honours had been joined by the Pesaro-based Benelli firm. This followed the Guzzi example by scoring an IOM TT victory when E.A. (Ted) Mellors won the Lightweight event at an average speed of almost 120 km/h (75 mph). This came after early leader Stanley Woods (Guzzi) retired after setting the fastest lap at 125.79 km/h (78.16 mph). Unlike Wood's Guzzi, the dohc Benelli had a vertical cylinder and no supercharging.

Blowers had come to the fore with a change in the ruling by the sport's international governing body, the FIM (Fédération Internationale Motocycliste). Guzzi, Gilera and Bianchi responded quickly and for the 1939 season all three fielded supercharged machines: the Guzzi was a blown version of its 250 single; the Gilera and Bianchi designs were 500 fours, the latter being an entirely new model. Benelli was also about to join the fray with a superbly crafted 250 four. Guzzi set its sights on racing a newly created 500 three-cylinder.

In practice, however, the era of the supercharged Grand Prix machine was brought to an abrupt halt when, on 3 September 1939, France and Britain declared war on Germany following the latter's invasion of Poland. Although Italy did not join the conflict until June 1940, international racing events ceased on that fateful September day. There then followed a period of over six years, when armaments took precedence over any other consideration, but at long last the war in Europe finally came to an end in May 1945.

The Immediate Post-War Period

Compared to its opposite numbers in Britain and Germany, the Italian motorcycle industry emerged relatively unscathed from the war. Only Benelli of the pre-war 'big four' had had its plant damaged by the Allied bombing raids and the retreating Germans.

Right: Tenni winning at Luino in 1945. His machine is one of the pre-war works 250 Moto Guzzi horizontal singles. The Guzzi factory at Mandello del Lario on the shores of Lake Como largely escaped damage in the Second World War, with the result that the company was one of the first in Italy to be able to resume peacetime activities.

Even so, only Guzzi and Gilera chose to resume their former competitive endeavours immediately the hostilities were over. Bianchi decided instead to concentrate its effort upon production, most of which was to be centred on its pedal cycle division.

Another factor was the FIM's ban on the use of superchargers or methanol fuel. This meant that the new high-performance Italian racing motorcycles designed and built in 1938-40 were effectively scrap metal. Exciting machines such as the 250 Benelli four, the 500 Bianchi four and the 500 Guzzi three were consigned to the metal crusher; and clean sheets of paper were rapidly sought. This affected everyone but the Italians most of all, as most of the British bikes were not supercharged and the Germans were in any case banned from competing outside their borders.

Luckily, the effects of the FIM ban were offset by the boom in the sale of standard production machines on the Italian home market in the years immediately following the end of the war. The revenue earned from these buoyant sales meant that the old-established marques could afford to commission new racing designs; and perhaps most important of all it allowed a whole host of new names to appear. The most significant of these were MV Agusta, FB Mondial, Morini and Parilla, all of whom came up with new and exciting racing models over the next few years.

With the introduction of a full-scale World Championship series for 125, 250, 350, 500 cc and sidecars from 1949, the scene was set for what is now referred to as the sport's Golden Era, the 1950s.

Right: Fergus Anderson in winning form aboard the Guzzi 500 cc V-twin during the very wet 1951 Swiss GP, held on the 7.27 kms (4.52 mile) Bremgarten circuit, Berne. His winning time of 1 hr 38 min 44.2 sec for the 28-lap race, at an average speed of 128.9 km/h (80.1 mph), was highly impressive. In its race report *Motor Cycle* commented, 'Anderson was riding in magnificent style. His Moto Guzzi appeared to handle as steadily as if the roads were dry and sounded in beautiful fettle!'

Italian Classic Gallery

World Champions

Italian bikes and riders made their mark from that very first year (1949) of the championships, for Nello Pagani took the 125 cc title on a Mondial, and Bruno Ruffo the 250 cc on a Guzzi. Up to and including the 1980 season, the combination of Italian motorcycle and rider scored another 42 championships, and there were many more by either the machine or rider alone.

Besides Pagani and Ruffo, other Italian World Champions who scored victories on Italian bikes are Carlo Ubbiali, Tarquinio Provini, Enrico Lorenzetti, Giacomo Agostini, Walter Villa, Pier Paolo Bianchi, Mario Lega, and Paolo Pileri.

Giacomo Agostini scored the largest number of victories: a total of 13 on MV Agusta machinery. This number added to the two he won on Yamahas, also makes him the rider with the greatest number of World titles in the history of road racing.

Style

Whatever else you may feel about Italian motorcycles, they have their own distinct attractiveness – what can only, and most emphatically, be called Style. Unlike some of the creations that have appeared in other countries, Italian bikes, and most certainly the racing variety, have the kind of looks that leave no one in any doubt as to their intended purpose; they exude their function.

As for colour, here again the Latin temperament comes into its own. Italian racing red has predominated, but there have been variations, many of them distinctive: bright orange Laverdas; green Patons, Guzzis and Benellis; and the very attractive blue and white Bianchi livery.

A Golden Era, Stagnation and Rebirth

The early and mid-1950s were without doubt not only the heyday of the Italian racing motorcycle, but arguably the Golden Era of the sport.

Several factors went to ensure this: record sales of production machines, fierce rivalry between factories for success on the race circuit, huge crowds of spectators throughout Europe, a full-scale World Championship series – the list is almost endless.

However, as with everything else in this life, the picture is not entirely without blemish. Accidents both to riders and spectators were to cause problems. The former was to deprive Italy of some of its finest postwar riding talent – men such as Dario Ambrosini, Carlo Maggi, Gianni Leoni and Sante Geminiani, all four of whom lost their lives within a few months during 1951, robbing Italy of potential future champions. In the same era others, such as Bruno Ruffo, suffered serious crashes that ended their careers. These tragedies were instrumental in opening the way for many of the established British and Commonwealth stars to join Italian factories. Without the need for replacements it is doubtful if factories like Guzzi, Gilera and MV Agusta would have signed men such as Duke, Armstrong, Kavanagh and Dale; and this recruitment in turn led to a host of others, including Surtees, Lomas, Campbell, Hocking and Hailwood.

The other aspect of the matter, accidents to spectators, was to prove vitally important in the history of Italian road racing. In this case what happened on four wheels, not two, was to be decisive for the future.

The carefree attitude of the racing fraternity was rudely shattered, first by the disaster in Le Mans 24 Hour event in 1955; and then by the equally horrendous incident during the Mille Miglia two years later. In both cases the problem centred around drivers loosing control of their cars and causing death within the massed ranks of spectators.

The first incident was to result in Italy's neighbour Switzerland promptly banning all forms of motor sport within its borders. The second signalled the end for the famous long-distance road races in Italy itself, such as the Moto Giro (Tour of Italy) and the Milano-Taranto.

All this could not have come at a worse time, as 1957 was also the year in which Gilera, Guzzi and Mondial decided jointly to withdraw from the sport. At the time, many could not understand the reasoning behind this decision; but it came in response to the rapidly declining sales of production roadsters, which had come about because of the growing sales of small family cars (headed by the Fiat 500) to an increasingly affluent customer.

Below: Back in 1950 Umberto Masetti had won the 500 cc World Championship for Gilera, a feat he repeated in 1952. He then left the Arcore company to join MV Agusta. But although a regular member of the team until he retired in 1957, he could never quite recapture his early form. He retired from racing and in 1958 went to live in Argentina; but in the early 1960s he contested the Grands Prix held in that country. He is shown here on the MV four at Faenza in 1956.

Another development, again during that fateful year of 1957, was the FIM's decision to ban the use of full streamlining. So as riders and spectators got ready for the 1958 season in Italy, it was a very different scene that greeted them: no long-distance marathons; all the big factories, with the exception of MV, now out of the programme; and the motorcycles themselves looking very different, either with much less

Italian Classic Gallery

Hailwood again in record-breaking form, this time at the Dutch TT, on 30 June 1964. He is shown here aboard his 500 MV Agusta on his way to not only another race victory but also a new circuit lap record at 144.76 km/h (89.95 mph).

A week of heatwave weather helped to ensure that yet another record was broken – before the racing had even started. Nearly 200,000 spectators were massed around the magnificently engineered circuit of nearly 8 km (5 miles) at Assen.

comprehensive 'dolphin' fairings, or completely naked machinery.

Italy, of course, was not alone in this. Much the same was happening throughout Europe, notably in Britain and Germany.

The events outlined above were to play into the hands of the emerging Japanese during the early 1960s, when machines with Honda, Suzuki and Yamaha inscribed on their petrol tanks began to make their presence felt, with ever greater vengeance with the passing of each year. Only MV Agusta, and to a much lesser extent the likes of Bianchi, Morini, Ducati and Benelli, prevented a total European whitewash in the World Championships.

By the middle of the decade, however, the Italians had at least started to fight back. First, Giacomo Agostini appeared on the scene. In 'Ago' the Italians at last had a rider capable of winning a title in the larger 350 and 500 cc classes. Anyone who witnessed the titanic battles between Agostini and his former MV teammate, Mike Hailwood (Honda) during 1966 and 1967 will need no reminder.

As the 1970s dawned, the Italian motorcycle industry staged something of a recovery. For the first time in many years, MV Agusta was joined by other names to present a real challenge to the dominant Japanese, not just at Grand Prix level,

Agostini in vivid action during the 1965 350 cc Italian Grand Prix at Monza. He won the 27-lap, 155.25 km (96.47 mile) event in 51 min 12.5 sec, an average speed of 181.90 km/h (113.03 mph).

Rain started towards the end of the race and one of several riders caught out was Agostini's team mate Hailwood, who slid off his MV while keeping 'team station' just astern of Ago. Later in the day Mike won the 500 cc race, but some idea of the slipperiness of the circuit can be gained from the fact that his average was 156.89 km/h (97.49 mph) –35 km/h (22 mph) under the previous year's winning speed!

but also in Formula 750, and other emerging production categories based on the superbike. Manufacturers such as Ducati, Guzzi and Laverda took part in these formulas, while Harley-Davidson (Aermacchi), Morbidelli, Villa and Malanca all mounted a challenge at World level in the smaller classes.

The 1970s also brought a move from Monza to Imola (and Mugello) for the Italian Grand Prix. This followed the fatal accident during the 250 cc Italian GP in 1973, which claimed the lives of Jarno Saarinen and Renzo Pasolini.

Towards the end of the decade (and the end of the period covered by this pictorial record of the Classic racing era, viewed from the Italian perspective) companies such as Garelli and Minerelli began to enter racing, together with Italy's 'new boys', Aprilia and Cagiva. However, ten years on we know with the benefit of hindsight that Japan, and not Italy, has dominated the 1980s in the World Championship series.

Will Italy, or indeed Europe, make a comeback? This must be the burning question for the 1990s.

Meanwhile enthusiasts will have to content themselves with the magnificent machines – and riders – contained within the following pages. These furnish proof that for many years Italy, was indisputably the dominant force in the world of motorcycle road racing.

THE MACHINES AND THE PLAYERS

4

Aermacchi

Although it never won a World title under its own name, Aermacchi is still important within the sphere of Italian road racing in the classic era. In addition, under the AMF Harley-Davidson label Aermacchi two-stroke twins gained four titles in the mid-1970s, with Walter Villa as rider.

Aermacchi, based in Varese, had a long history, but much of it was in aviation. It was not until 1950 that Aermacchi entered the two-wheel field.

For the first ten years it concentrated its efforts on roadsters, albeit with the odd offroad or record-breaker thrown in. Then in 1960 two important things happened. The first was a financial tie-up with the American Harley-Davidson company; the second the firm's racing début. The latter came when teenager Alberto Pagani finished 9th in the Dutch TT on what was essentially a converted roadster. A week later in Belgium he did even better with a 5th place. Spurred on by this success, Aermacchi decided to build 'over-the-counter' versions for sale to private customers.

Although the various capacities of this humble pushrod single never won a Grand Prix, they none the less formed the backbone of privateer racing during the mid-1960s, between the demise of the British singles and the introduction of the Yamaha TD and TR twins.

Realizing the limitations of the design, the Varese concern then made a move into two-strokes. First came a 125 single in 1968, followed two years later by the prototype of the twin-cylinder model that was to prove so successful in later years.

World Championships: 250 cc 1974, 1975 and 1976; 350 cc 1976

Imola, Sunday 15 April 1962. British star John Hartle on holiday in Italy, still sidelined with a broken arm, studies Gilberto Milani's works 250 Aermacchi. In the race Milani finished 4th behind Tom Phillis and Jim Redman on Honda fours and Walter Tassinari on one of the super-fast works Morini singles of the type used by Tarquinio Provini.

Aermacchi

Left: Tommy Robb (12) and Brian Clark (61) on their production Ala d'Oros contest the lead in Heat 1 of the 250 cc event on the hairpin at Mallory Park, on 10 June 1962. They went on to finish 3rd and 5th respectively in the final, which was won by the Honda team captain Jim Redman on one of the Japanese four-cylinder models.

Bottom far left: The 1963 Southern 100 races run over the 7.9 km (4.4 mile) Billown Circuit near Castletown, Isle of Man, saw a classic fight for victory between the 250 cc winner Terry Grotefeld (51) and runner-up Jim Curry (37). The two riders had almost identical Aermacchis. Grotefeld's winning time for the nine-lap race was 30 min 22.6 sec, a speed of 121.57 km/h (75.54 mph).

Bottom left: The production Aermacchi (1962) wet-clutch 246.2 cc (66 x 72 mm) Ala d'Oro racing engine. Although fast, it was far from reliable. The most common sources of trouble were the big end and connecting rod.
This engine with pushrod-operated valves delivered 28 bhp at the rear wheel at 9800 rpm, with good torque from around 6700 rpm. The gearbox was a four-speeder, with a wet clutch.

Above right: By 1964 the 250 Aermacchi sported not only revised looks, but shorter stroke measurements of 72 x 61 mm, and power raised to 28 bhp at 9500 rpm. In 1965 this figure was increased to 30 bhp at 10,000 rpm, and a dry clutch fitted. The latter change can be identified by the ventilated cover (sometimes removed) on the right-hand (offside) of the power unit. Completing the picture were Oldani racing brakes, Ceriani front forks and attractive glassfibre ware.

Right: The first four-stroke home in the 1965 Lightweight Manx Grand Prix was Colin Fenton's Aermacchi in 4th place. He completed the four-lap, 60.75 km (37.75 mile) Mountain course in 1 hr 44 min 26.4 sec, an average speed of 139.56 km/h (86.72 mph). Fenton had been fourth quickest in practice, and was also the first rider away as the maroon banged its signal to the 96 starters. The race was run in perfect weather conditions and all four of the leading quartet bettered the 1964 race speeds.

Italian *Classic* Gallery

One of the two double overhead camshaft Aermacchi engines built in the mid-1960s. This is the works version, which featured gear drive to the cams – this necessitated a longer crankshaft and outside flywheel. Besides this prototype there was a privately built version conceived by Celestino Piva, an employee of the Aermacchi factory. Both are now owned by a Swiss enthusiast, Yves Liengme (he was the Swiss importer during most of the 1960s). Maximum power was 35 bhp and the unit would run up to more than 13,000 rpm.

Below left: Monza, Sunday 14 September 1966. Factory riders Renzo Pasolini (left, without helmet) and Alberto Pagani. Both have Aermacchi 350s, but with different streamlining. The pair had just finished a brilliant 2nd and 3rd respectively in the 350 cc Italian Grand Prix. Works Bianchi and Jawa twins finished behind them in what was probably Aermacchi's finest GP success.

Opposite top left: A 1967 model production 344 cc (74 x 80 mm) Ala d'Oro. Note the non-standard clutch cover modification, also the SAFA battery, rear engine mounting, padding for tank, remote float chamber and waisted fairing. The maximum power output was now up to 40 bhp at 7800 rpm.

Opposite top right: The 1968 250 and 350 Ala D'Oros looked like this, with Fontana brakes, new glassfibre, 35 mm Ceriani forks and a generally superb finish. By now these bikes were extremely reliable: more than could be said of the earlier versions.

Right: Works rider Alberto Pagani in action in 1968 on the prototype 123 cc (56 x 50 mm) single-cylinder Aermacchi two-stroke. This differed from the later bikes by having an iron cylinder barrel, four-speed gearbox and no front frame downtube.

Aermacchi

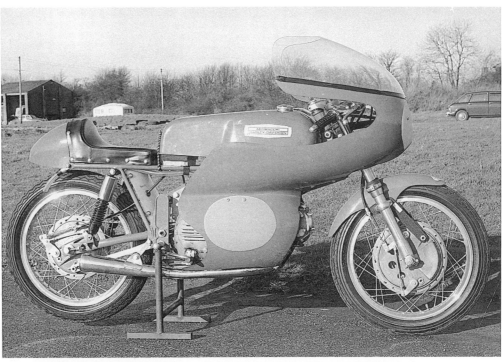

Italian *Classic* Gallery

Kel Carruthers, who was the 1969 250 cc World Champion (for Benelli), also rode Aermacchis in both the 125 and 350 cc classes. Here he is seen on the larger machine in the Junior TT that year. After being well placed he was forced to retire; while on the smaller two-stroke model he finished 2nd to race winner Dave Simmonds on a works Kawasaki.

Inset: In the Austrian Grand Prix, on 1 May 1969, Gilberto Milani heads the field in the 350 cc race on his fast factory bike. Note the cobblestones, and how close the spectators are – neither would be tolerated today.

Above: Following the success of its 125 cc two-stroke, Aermacchi management decided upon a new 250 (and later 350) cc twin-cylinder 'stroker to replace its by now ageing pushrod singles. The first prototype shown here was tested by works rider Renzo Pasolini in 1970. The engine was essentially a pair of the 125 singles in a common crankcase.

Left: The 1970 version of the two-stroke Aermacchi-Harley-Davidson 125 racer. With improved porting, 28 mm carburettor and five-speed gearbox, its 22 bhp at 9200 rpm was good for well over 177 km/h (110 mph) on optimum gearing. Dry weight was a mere 80 kg (176 lb).

Opposite top: Crankshaft, ignition and tachometer drive details of the 1972 250 Aermacchi racing twin. Note the seals and cotterpin crank coupling. The ignition system was made by Dansi, a firm that, like Aermacchi, was based in Varese.

Below right: The six-speed gearbox showing the housing and cluster.

Bottom: Aermacchi works rider Alberto Pagani. The son of former Gilera and Mondial works star Nello, Alberto began his racing career in 1959 on a 125 Ducati. His first Aermacchi ride came in 1960 on the prototype 250 flat single racer. He was to ride for the Varese factory for over 10 years before ultimately joining MV Agusta in the early 1970s to team up with Phil Read.

Bottom middle: Hero of Varese: Renzo ('Paso') Pasolini, the bespectacled star who had earlier ridden the Aermacchi flat singles as well as the four-cylinder Benellis, soon began to make an impact on the new two-strokes. By 1972 the machines were competitive and against a horde of Yamahas he had wins in the Italian, Yugoslav and Spanish 250 cc GPs.

Bottom right: Walter Villa was born at Modena on 13 August 1943 and made his racing debut on a Morini Setabello 175 in 1964. The younger brother of the former Ducati works rider Francesco, Walter gained experience by racing a wide range of machinery, including Mondial and Montesa two-strokes; four-cylinder works Benellis; and even 750s in the shape of a Triumph Trident and Kawasaki threes.

Italian *Classic* Gallery

Harley–Davidson

Right inset: Engine details from the 250 cc Harley-Davidson, the type that Walter Villa rode to take the World Championship in 1974, 1975 and 1976. Clearly visible are the water-cooled head and barrels, radiator, Dell'Orto carburettors, clutch operating arm and Dansi electronic ignition system. By 1976 the 246 cc engine was producing 58 bhp at 12,000 rpm; the larger 347 cc unit was good for 70 bhp at 11,400 rpm. Maximum speeds were 250 km/h (155 mph) and 266 km/h (165 mph) respectively.

The 250 cc Czech GP 1977. Walter Villa (1) leads Tom Herron, Yamaha (5); Korky Ballington, Kawasaki (15); and Alan North, Yamaha (22). Although he had victories in Venezuela, Italy, Belgium and Finland, Villa lost the title to the more consistent Mario Lega with the Morbidelli – even though Lega only won a single Grand Prix. Villa finished the season in third spot in the Championship series, with new team mate Franco Uncini in the runner-up position. At the end of the year the factory withdrew its support and 1978 saw a disastrous spell under the sponsorship of the Nolan helmet company. Subsequently Villa left to ride his own privately entered Yamahas.

Far right inset: Walter Villa in action during his winning ride in the 1976 250 cc West German Grand Prix at Hockenheim. He won from team mate Michel Rougerie and Yamaha star Victor Palomo. Note the Campagnolo enclosed disc brake at the front and square section swinging arm.

Italian *Classic* Gallery

Benelli

Until 1960, Benelli successes were chiefly associated with the names of two great riders: Ted Mellors and Dario Ambrosini. It was Mellors who first brought the company into prominence when, riding the only Benelli in the race, he won the 1939 Lightweight TT in the face of very stiff opposition. His Manx victory on the single-cylinder Pesaro-built machine created a sensation in racing circles long used to DKW and Guzzi domination of the 250 cc class.

Later, in 1950, Benelli again sprang to the attention of racing enthusiasts when Ambrosini beat the all-conquering Guzzis to win the 250 cc Individual World Championship for himself, and the Manufacturer's award for the company. Unfortunately, however, Ambrosini was Benelli so far as racing was concerned, and when he was killed practising for the 1951 French Grand Prix, the factory virtually retired from the sport.

In 1959, however, Benelli returned with a new edition of its long-running double camshaft single, with Geoff Duke, Dickie Dale and Silvio Grassetti as riders.

The following year the company made headlines by testing a completely new 250 four. In practice this design was not raced until 1962. Success finally came at the end of the decade when the Australian Kel Carruthers became Benelli's second World Champion in 1969.

The marque retired from sport in 1972 after being taken over by the Argentinian industrialist, Alejandro de Tomaso.

World Championships: 250 cc 1950 and 1969

Ambrosini seen here at Kirkmichael in the 1950 Lightweight TT, on his way to victory. On the last lap he set a new record of 27 min. 59 secs., 80.91 mph. This photograph perfectly captures the atmosphere of the Island in the early post-war period.

Above right: The engine from Dario Ambrosini's 248.8 cc (65 x 75 mm) double overhead camshaft Benelli single. This 1949 shot shows the unit to be little changed from the original pre-war engine as used by Ted Mellors to win the 1939 Lightweight TT. Drive to the overhead cams was by a train of gears. Lubrication was of the dry sump variety; the oil tank and oil cooler are clearly visible. Note also the separate gearbox and the mass of external oil pipes.

Above left: The smiling face of Dario Ambrosini at the Lightweight TT in 1950, which he won. The Benelli ace had been runner-up to this World title in 1949, and was to finish in 3rd place in 1951, the year in which he was to meet his death during practice for the French Grand Prix in July. His accident was attributed to his skidding on tar that had melted in scorching sunshine. This caused the brilliant Italian to lose control and collide with a telegraph pole; he died almost instantly from his injuries.

Left: Seen from above the Benelli four-cylinder engine is an impressive piece of machinery, with its mass of plug leads, oil and fuel pipes, its four carburettors and ignition coils. Partly visible to the far left of the photograph is the distributor, which denotes this as the original prototype tested in 1960 and 1961 with coil ignition.

Right: Following Ambrosini's untimely death Benelli gave up racing until 1959, when updated versions of the venerable 250 single were ridden by Dickie Dale, Geoff Duke and the dashing young Italian Silvio Grassetti (shown here at Monza with one of the revised machines). The most notable differences were in the running gear, the new frame, telescopic forks, full-width hub brakes and a dolphin fairing.

First unveiled in June 1960, the 250 four-cylinder Benelli did not make its race début until 15 April 1962, at Imola. With works rider Silvio Grassetti in the saddle, it held 3rd place until stopped by gearbox trouble, after eight laps. Lack of funds were to restrict its development.

Italian *Classic* Gallery

Above left: Nearside view of the early 1962 Benelli engine, showing magneto, cylinder head and exposed dry clutch to advantage. With bore and stroke measurements of 44 x 40.5 mm, it displaced 246.3 cc. Maximum power from the gear-driven double overhead camshaft engine was around 40 bhp. This was about 5 bhp less than the comparable Honda design.

Above: The Benelli four in the Pesaro factory with Paolo Benelli (right) and ex-Ducati mechanic Armoroli, March 1962.

Left: Benelli's 1962 type 250 four-cylinder engine. Note the massive sump, forward mounted magneto and neatly crafted crankcases and clutch assembly. The full duplex frame provided excellent roadholding and handling.

Benelli

Right: Lakeside action as Mike Hailwood pilots the Fron Purslow-sponsored 250 Benelli to victory on the opening day of the British road-racing season at Mallory Park, on 1 April 1962. Later, on the same machine, Hailwood was destined to be in a secure 4th place in the Lightweight TT behind a trio of works Hondas, only to retire on the last lap with engine trouble.

Below: Fairing-off view of the Benelli four used by Grassetti of Imola in April 1962. Compared with the original prototype there were several changes. The ignition system was altered from coil to magneto. This was mounted forward of the engine with the armature shaft in line with the direction of travel, and driven by skew gears from the crankshaft. The oil was now contained in a sump instead of an oil tank (which on the prototype was mounted forward of the petrol tank). An Oldani front brake was fitted instead of one of Benelli's own design as on the earlier singles.

One-ji rivals must have all them suffered perhaps the biggest shock of their 250 cc World Championship career at the Spanish GP on 6 May 1962. That Sunday was when Italy's Silvio Grassetti on the new four-cylinder Benelli hounded Jim Redman, Tom Phillis and Bob McIntyre for lap after lap of the gruelling Montjuich Park circuit in Barcelona. Grassetti actually caught and passed the Scottish ace, breaking the lap record in the process, before his Benelli coasted to a standstill with engine trouble after 24 laps of the 33 lap, 125.9 km (78.24 mile) race.

This was the Pesaro-built four's first appearance in a World Championship event and came less than a week after Grassetti had given the machine its first victory, at the International meeting on 1 May at Cesenatico, Italy.

Benelli

Above: The Fron Purslow Benelli at Silverstone in early 1963 minus its fairing. Among its technical details note the Amal carburettor, twin Bosch ignition coils, dry clutch, exposed hairpin valve springs, and exhaust cam-driven tachometer drive.

The great Tarquinio Provini with what was to be the final version of the Benelli 250 single-cylinder racer, at the American GP, March 1964. Pitted against the latest Yamaha twins of Itoh and Duff, the by now ageing Italian single was hopelessly outclassed, and so it was retired from active duty.

Italian *Classic* Gallery

Tarquinio Provini joined Benelli from Morini at the end of 1963. Although improvements were made, and Provini won the Spanish GP that year, it was not enough and his replacement in the Morini team, Giacomo Agostini, won the Italian Championship. However, with Agostini going to MV Agusta, Provini and Benelli took the Italian title in 1965. Our photograph shows Provini in March that year testing a new dual disc hydraulic front brake on the Modena circuit.

Below: Renzo Pasolini in winning form at Modena in 1967 on the new 491 cc Benelli four. He beat multi-World Champion Giacomo Agostini's three-cylinder MV Agusta by a nose after a sensational race. In the races held along the Italian Adriatic coast, Pasolini managed to beat the champion several times that year, especially in the 350 cc class. In the World Championship, however, it was Agostini and MV who led the way.

Silvio Grassetti made a triumphant return to the Benelli camp at the Italian Grand Prix at Monza in September 1967. In the 350 race he rode one of the Pesaro fours into 2nd place behind Ralph Bryans' Honda six-cylinder. By that time the 343.1 cc (51 x 42 mm) model was delivering over 60 bhp at 14,000 rpm.

Right: Drafted into the Benelli team to replace the injured Pasolini, the Australian Kel Carruthers promptly won his first race for the company: no less than the extremely demanding Isle of Man Tourist Trophy. Following Yamaha's withdrawal from works participation at the end of 1968, Benelli had decided to concentrate its efforts on the 250 cc class; but the first three rounds of the 1969 World Championship were dominated by Santiago Herrero (Ossa) and Kent Anderson (Yamaha). However, with Carruthers' arrival on the scene, things changed rapidly with victories in the Ulster Grand Prix (illustrated) and in Yugoslavia to add to that in the Manx TT, and also a number of other leaderboard placings. This gave Benelli its second World Championship (Dario Ambrosini had won the first back in 1950).

Italian *Classic* Gallery

Main picture: Walter Villa on the 350 Benelli four with which he finished 5th in the Italian GP at Monza on 20 May 1973. This photograph is significant for the fact that the fatal accident suffered by Renzo Pasolini and Jarno Saarinen is generally attributed to oil left on the circuit by Villa's Benelli (although it must be said that the race officials were to blame in not acting to prevent the tragedy in the 250 cc race, which was held directly after the end of the 350 cc event). Villa was to take Pasolini's place in the Aermacchi-Harley-Davidson team and go on to win four world titles.

Below: The 1969 250 cc World Champion Kel Carruthers with his wife and, *far right,* Mimo Benelli the factory's racing manager. Carruthers, born 3 January 1938, achieved numerous successes on Honda, Norton and Aermacchi machines as a privateer. His wide experience proved invaluable to Benelli, where he provided the consistency that had previously been lacking.
In the closely contested 1969 season, only the final event could determine the World Championship: Carruthers was equal to the occasion and won.

Above inset: For 1970 Carruthers was forced to ride a Yamaha, rather than a Benelli, in the 250 cc class. This was because of the FIM's new ruling that year limiting the class to a maximum of two cylinders and six gears (the 1969 Benelli four had *eight* gears). However, for the Isle of Man the Pesaro factory provided the Australian star with one of its latest 350s. With 64 bhp at 14,500 rpm and a maximum speed of over 250 km/h (160 mph), this machine looked set to offer an effective challenge to the dominant Agostini and his MV. The duel, however, never took place. At the end of the first lap the Benelli rider was lying 2nd, but some 70 seconds adrift, and over 3 minutes by the end of the third. In the following lap Carruthers had problems and retired at Ramsey.

Italian *Classic* Gallery

Bianchi

More famous for its pre-Second World War activities than for its postwar endeavours, this old-established Milanese company none the less fielded works machines from 1959 to 1965.

At first these employed single-cylinder overhead camshaft engines developed from the Bianchi motocrossers. Then for 1960 chief designer Ing. Lino Tonti produced an all-new dohc 250 twin. Unfortunately, this suffered problems of both excess weight and marginal reliability. However, Tonti and Bianchi pressed on, and for 1961 the design was revamped as a 350. This solved the power-to-weight ratio, but the machine was still afflicted by an excessive number of retirements. For example, of no fewer than five works Bianchi twins that came to the line at the 1961 Italian GP, only one, ridden by Alan Shepherd, finished. Even so Ernesto Brambilla took the 500 Senior Italian Championship with one of the 350 cc Bianchis that year.

The design was carefully developed between 1961 and 1964. Remo Venturi scored a number of leader board places at both home Internationals and on the Grand Prix circuit, and this culminated with the same rider taking the 500 cc Italian Senior Championship title in 1964. By then the larger capacity machine was a full 500, after being given gradual increases in capacity from the original 350, a slightly overbored 352 cc.

World Championships: None

Bianchi returned to road racing, after a long lay-off, with a new 250 single in 1959. This was developed from the successful motocross machines. Ing. Lino Tonti had noticed how good the power curve was and the result was a modified unit for tarmac events. With a new frame, brakes and other cycle parts, the new bike made its debut at the Swiss GP (by then a non-championship event) at Locarno. Rider Gianfranco Muscio recorded some very respectable times before being put out of the race with valve spring trouble.

Bianchi

Top left inset: The Bianchi single-cylinder overhead camshaft, unit construction engine. For road racing it was produced in two engine sizes: 248 cc (77 x 53.4 mm) and 174 cc (65 x 52.6 mm). Claimed output was 20 bhp at 10,500 rpm for the 175 and 30 bhp at 10,000 rpm for the larger unit. The two shared details such as straight-cut primary drive gears, close ratio gear clusters, wet sump lubrication, twin ignition coils and Oldani brakes. Their development, however, was cut short after Ing. Tonti was told by the company's management to proceed with the design of a new 250 twin-cylinder model for Grand Prix events.

Main picture: Bianchi works rider Ernesto Brambilla leads Britain's Phil Read (Norton) during the 1961 Dutch TT on the Assen circuit. They finished the race in 4th and 5th places respectively. Bob McIntyre on another of the Bianchi twins came home an impressive 2nd to the race victor Gary Hocking (MV Agusta Four). The Czech Jawa rider Franta Stastny was in 3rd place, between the Bianchi pair.

Bottom left inset: After building their new 250 twin for the 1960 season, Ing. Lino Tonti and Bianchi soon found it too large and heavy. Tonti therefore replaced this late in 1960 with a 348.4 cc (70 x 59 mm) which offered a much superior power-to-weight ratio. With the choice of five- or six-speed transmission, the larger-engined twin was capable of a fine performance – around 240 km/h (150 mph), but was hampered at first by poor reliability. The 1961 version is illustrated.

Italian *Classic* Gallery

Left: Besides McIntyre there was another Scot, Alastair King, who rode for the Milanese factory during 1961. He is shown here finishing 2nd (behind Gary Hocking's MV) in the Ulster Grand Prix, at an average speed of 148.54 km/h (92.30 mph). This was to be his only finish on the machine.

Below: The 1964 498 cc Bianchi twin. Its best placing in a classic event that year was Remo Venturi's 2nd in the Dutch TT; at home the Italian veteran proved his worth by winning the national 500 cc title. However, things were going from bad to worse on the commercial front for Bianchi and at the end of the year Venturi left.

Right: Silvio Grassetti was able to ride the latest version of the Bianchi 350 twin in 1965 simply because he met his racing expenses out of his own pocket. He is shown here at the Dutch TT at Assen, where in practice he had been fourth fastest (behind Hailwood and Agostini on MV Agustas, and Jim Redman's Honda). He held this position in the race until lap 13, when he retired. Later in the season his luck changed with a runner's-up placing at Monza on the same bike.

Remo Venturi at Imola, Easter 1964. That year he rode 350 and 500 Bianchi twins to win the Senior Italian Championship. By this time the Bianchis were not only the fastest twin-cylinder four-strokes around, but reliable too. The larger engine had been developed first from an overbored 350 to 422, then 454 and 482, until in 1964 it was up to 498.06 cc (73 x 59.5 mm). As a full 500 the Bianchi gave 72 bhp at 10,200 rpm.

Italian *Classic* Gallery

Bimota

One of the early Bimotas was this Paton-engined machine ridden by Amando Corecca in 1973. It employed a development of the double overhead camshaft unit designed by ex-Mondial engineer Giuseppe Pattoni. The 498 cc two-valve engine produced 65 bhp at 10,500 rpm, which was not enough to challenge the MV Agusta, or the new two-strokes such as the Yamaha or Kawasaki.

Left: The rising star Johnny Cecotto from Venezuela used a Bimota frame in 1975 to win the 350 cc World Championship. Cecotto had victories in Belgium, France, West Germany, Italy and Finland.

Giuseppe Elementi was the first rider to win Bimota
international acclaim with his outstanding results on a Bimota-
framed Yamaha 350 in 1974. Elementi won many races in Italy
that year, and finished an excellent 7th in the Italian GP at
Imola.

Bimota

Left: First test of the Bimota-Morbidelli 250. Housed in a special Bimota monoshock chassis, the Jörg Möller-designed 249.7 cc (56 x 50.7 mm) disc valve twin-cylinder engine pumped out 64 bhp at 11,500 rpm, and was good for around 260 km/h (over 160 mph). This photograph shows its appearance at Modena in the spring of 1976. *Left to right:* Mori, Diongi, Tamburini, and rider Pier Paolo Bianchi. *Opposite bottom left:* This all-new Bimota racer made its bow in March 1976. It was powered by a four-carburettor twin-cylinder Harley-Davidson 500 cc engine. Ridden by Vanes Francini, the official Bimota rider, it was extremely fast, but generally its engine was temperamental. Unfortunately, Harley-Davidson at its Varese factory was already fully occupied with the 250 and 350 cc racers of its own team headed by Walter Villa. Although offering 90 bhp, the six-speed water-cooled 500 cc motor was abandoned later that year. *Below:* The Italian Suzuki importers commissioned Bimota to build a batch of 50 TR 500-engined racers. The result was the Bimota SB Saiad Suzuki TR 500. These employed a 492 cc (70 x 64 mm) twin-cylinder unit. Running on a 6.4:1 compression ratio and with Mikuni carburettors, power output was 83 bhp at 9000 rpm. Besides a Bimota frame, the specification included 18 in Bimota magnesium wheels, Brembo disc brakes and Ceriani forks. Dry weight was 121 kg (267 lb).

Opposite bottom right: The Bimota drawing office in 1977. By then the Rimini concern was well known for its creative design and its engineering flair. The success of the Bimota racing chassis led to the company becoming a world-famous name. It also enabled it to develop into a specialist manufacturer of exclusive (and expensive!) superbikes powered by Japanese multi-cylinder engines, for both road and track.

Capriolo

The Milan-Taranto event 1956. This Capriolo took part in the Series Production 75 cc class. Note the massive tank, pressed steel frame and offset carburettor. The engine employed a face cam — a feature of this famous marque.

Italian *Classic* Gallery

Ceccato

Orlando Ghiro, a factory tester at the Ceccato works, assumes the prone position on his 75 cc, fully streamlined model. He broke four world speed records in both the 75 and 100 cc categories on 1 January 1955. Over the 1 mile flying start Ghiro clocked 134.672 km/h (83.5 mph). He also set new records for the 1 km flying start and the standing start at both distances.

The Ceccato engine was a chain-driven overhead camshaft single; this was also used to good effect in long-distance road races.

Ducati

Seldom has a marque made a more dramatic entry into racing than Ducati. For not only did the Bologna concern win its first big race – the 1956 125 cc Swedish Grand Prix – but its victorious single-cylinder machine was the first in the history of the sport to feature an engine with desmodromic (positively operated) valves. Tragically Degli Antoni, winner of the Swedish race, was fatally injured shortly afterwards while practising for the Italian GP at Monza. This set the company and its gifted designer, Ing. Fabio Taglioni, back a full year. The result was that a proper challenge could not be set in motion until 1958. Yet what a year that was, for against the toughest opposition Ducati works riders Gandossi and Spaggiari won three of the season's main 125 cc events. In the Italian Grand Prix, the last classic of the year, Ducatis took the first five places: much to the chagrin of their main rivals, the mighty MV Agusta team!

Francesco Villa, who finished 3rd at Monza, was riding a new desmodromic twin-cylinder model. This subsequently became the basis of two larger twins; a 'one-off' 250 cc machine built to the special order of the wealthy Englishman Stan Hailwood for the exclusive use of his son, Mike; and an exciting 350.

The 1959 season was less successful for Ducati than 1958 had been, for the company won only one of the big events, the 125 cc Ulster Grand Prix.

Since then Ducati has concentrated its efforts upon events where production-based machinery is used, rather than on attempts for Grand Prix honours. For example, it has won the prestigious Barcelona 24 Hours race more times than any other manufacturer; scored a sensational 1st and 2nd in the inaugural Imola 200 against the cream of the world's superbikes; and taken four TT Formula 2 World titles in the 1980s.

World Championships: None (in the classic period)

Opposite top: An extremely rare photograph taken in England, at Blandford Army Camp on 6 February 1955, showing six Britax Hurricane 50 racers. These used a Ducati Cucciolo ('Little Pup') pullrod four-stroke engine and were significant for two things: their full alloy 'dustbin' fairing, and a distinct lack of performance!

Right: One of the very first of Ing. Fabio Taglioni's 124 cc (55.25 x 52 mm) single-cylinder Desmos. This is evident from the early style of frame and the type of air scoop fitted to the Amadoro double-sided front brake. The type shown was intended for use with the fully enclosed streamlining that was banned by the FIM at the end of the 1957 season. The 125 Desmo single made its winning debut at the 1956 Swedish Grand Prix at Hedemora, when works rider Gianni Degli Antoni lapped the entire field.

Italian *Classic* Gallery

Grand Prix des Nations, Monza, 14 September 1958. The supporting 175 cc Formula 3 race was won by Ducati rider Francesco Villa (shown with the victor's spoils). The Motobi riders Muscio and Sala were 2nd and 3rd respectively. The same day the Ducati factory scored its greatest ever Grand Prix triumph by scooping the first *five* places in the 125 cc event.

Irishman Sammy Miller (later to become the world's premier trials competitor) was one of four works riders entered for Ducati in the 1958 Isle of Man 125 cc TT. It was run over the 17.28 km (10.79 mile) Clypse Circuit and Miller took 4th place after averaging 113.35 km/h (70.43 mph) on his desmodromic single.

Engine assembly from the 125 Formula 3 machine. This shared its engine dimensions with the more sophisticated double overhead camshaft Grand Prix model and even the works desmodromic singles. Unlike them, however, it employed only one camshaft and a four-speed gearbox. In fact, at least externally, the engine was almost identical to the standard production 125 Sport (Monza in Britain). The only give-aways were the rev counter drive, larger Dell'Orto SS1 racing carburettor, externally mounted condenser, oil pipes and the sand cast engine covers. The Formula 3 racers were built from 1958 to 1961.

A batch of 25 125 cc Ducati Formula 3 machines at the company's Bologna factory in January 1959. Together with a larger 175 cc version, these machines gave many riders in Italy their first taste of competition. However, in export markets such as Britain their high price restricted sales to a trickle. Today they are worth a small fortune to knowledgeable collectors.

Australian star Ken Kavanagh rode Ducati machinery in the twilight of a brilliant career, which had seen him on works bikes from Norton, Moto Guzzi and MV Agusta. He is shown here at Nursery Bends on his double overhead camshaft Grand Prix single in the 125 cc Lightweight TT, 3 June 1959. Holding 5th place early in the race behind Ubbiali (MV Agusta), Hailwood (Ducati), Provini (MV Agusta) and Taveri (MZ), he suffered problems with a blocked fuel tank cap vent and, trying to open the cap, damaged the neck of the orifice. Fuel gushed out as soon as the machine was on the move, and so Kavanagh was forced into an early retirement.

Ducati's first twin was this 174 cc model designed by Ing. Taglioni in 1956. The 49.4 x 45.6 mm bore and stroke valve-spring engine had four speeds. Running on a compression ratio of 10.2:1 it gave a claimed 25 bhp at an ear-splitting 11,000 rpm, and had a top speed of some 170 km/h (105 mph). It was intended mainly for events such as the Milan-Taranto and Giro d'Italia. Unfortunately, both these events were banned in 1957 following the Mille Miglia tragedy. In circuit events the design was at a distinct disadvantage, being both overweight and up against full 250s. The particular machine shown was sent to Britain in early 1959 for Mike Hailwood. However, it was soon withdrawn and in its place a full 250 cc version with desmodromic valve operation appeared.

Italian *Classic* Gallery

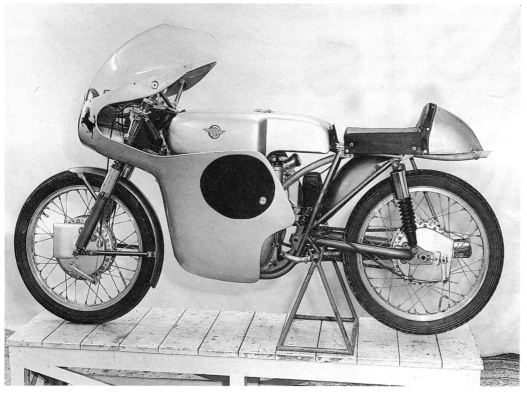

Ridden by riders of the calibre of Spaggiari and Hailwood, the 1959 version of Ing. Taglioni's superb 125 Desmo single could match the works MV Agustas, but an inconsistent approach to the World Championship series ruined Ducati's chances. However, Hailwood won the Ulster GP (his first GP victory) and took 3rd place in the Isle of Man and Dutch TTs and the German GP, with 4th in the Swedish round. One of Mike's two identical bikes is illustrated.

Below: British rider Brian Clark with the Ducati 175 Formula 3 he rode in the 1959 250 cc TT. He was lying in 10th spot when a crash put him out of the running. At the end of the year Tom Lambert, his father-in-law and sponsor (with him in the picture), approached Alan Mullee of the Manchester-based Ducati importers about a five-speed gearbox. The result was that the engine went to the factory, where not only did it receive an extra cog, but also a double-knocker head. In 1960 it took Clark to victory in the Scottish 200 cc Championship. For 1961 it was converted to 198 cc by replacing the original 62 mm piston with a 66 mm Hepolite component. Throughout the year the machine was fast enough for a good number of top placings, highlighted by a 2nd position behind Shorey's NSU Sportmax at the Scarborough International in September.

Opposite: The engine unit from Mike Hailwood's 250 Desmo twin. Its specification included: 249.7 cc (55.25 x 52 mm); gear-operated triple overhead camshafts, driven by a train of gears between the two cylinders; ignition battery/coil; six-speed gearbox. Maximum power was 43 bhp at 11,600 rpm, which provided a top speed of around 218 km/h (135 mph). Although more powerful than any other twin-cylinder racer at the time (the MV Agusta twin gave 37 bhp), the Ducati design suffered from a very narrow power band, under-development and excess weight.

Italian *Classic* Gallery

Top left: Arthur Wheeler piloting his Ducati 125 double overhead camshaft Grand Prix model at Thruxton in the summer of 1961. He rode this machine (and later an ex-factory Desmo) on both the British short circuits, and the Continental Grand Prix Circus, complementing his larger Moto Guzzi flat singles.

Above: The great Mike Hailwood at Silverstone on 4 April, 1960, about to test his new 250 Ducati Desmo twin. His father Stan was then head of the Kings of Oxford chain of motorcycle dealers and had established a subsidiary, Ducati Concessionaires, to import the Ducati range into Britain. He also commissioned the manufacture by Ducati of 250 (and 350) machines for use by Mike, to complement the 125 Desmo singles on which he had won the 1959 ACU Star. Unfortunately, the 250 and 350 Desmo twins were destined to become two of the very few failures of Ing. Taglioni's long reign.

Left: The diminutive R.G.J. (Gary) Dickinson was one of the leading competitors using a Ducati 125 GP in the early 1960s. In fact, he was so tiny that he was forced to carry ballast to meet FIM weight regulations! However, this did not stop Dickinson from putting up some truly excellent performances. He found the annual Southern 100 races particularly to his liking. These were held over the Billown Circuit near Castletown, Isle of Man. The photograph shows him riding to 2nd place in the 1961 125 cc event. The following year he did even better and won.

Welshman Mick Manley leads Heat 1 of the 250 cc event at Aberdare Park in August 1962. Mechanical trouble put him out of the final. Even so his performances earned him the runner-up spot in the 250 cc ACU Star (British Championship) that year. His machine was one of only half a dozen 220s – actually 216.130 cc (69 x 57.8 mm) – double overhead camshaft Ducati singles to be built. Based on the production 175 Formula 3 racer, the 220 featured a double-knocker head, and also a five-speed box. Manley's bike was finished in a distinctive gold colour and was one of the very few machines that year to challenge the Aermacchi Ala d'Oro on the British short circuits.

After the Hailwood équipe disposed of its Desmo twins at the end of 1960 they were acquired by John Surtees. The former MV Agusta star and World Champion kept all the 350s, but disposed of two 250s. One went to Londoner Jim Russell. Sponsored by Pullin Motors of Dulwich, Russell achieved a number of excellent results in the period 1963-64. One of the few important changes he made was to fit the front brake from a Manx Norton. In Russell's hands the infamous twin at last proved its worth. The photograph shows Jim Russell in action at Brands Hatch on Sunday 13 October 1963, on the Druids Hill bend. Against top-class opposition he finished 7th.

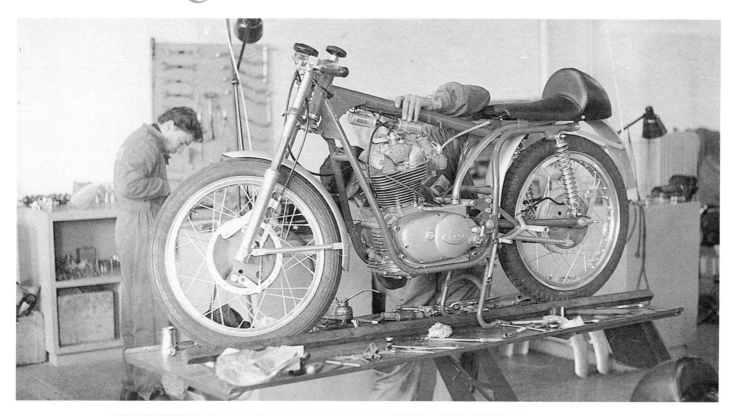

Above: One of the 250 Mach 1/S racers derived from the Barcelona 24 Hours winner of 1964. Built in 1965 and 1966 (shown here), these bikes were exceedingly reliable, but much too heavy for success on the short circuits. The 250 gave 30 bhp at 10,500 rpm; the 350 version pumped out 38 bhp at 9000 rpm. Cylinder heads were of the conventional valve spring type, not desmodromic.

Engine unit of the 250 Mach 1/S. Note the visible differences between this and 'narrow-case' production 250 Ducati of the era. These include much wider engine mounts, sand cast covers, different clutch cover, larger sump, larger crankcases and duplex frame. Note the blanked-off kickstart pivot.

Ducati

In the mid-1960s Ducati built this Taglioni-designed, jewel of a 125 four-cylinder model. Unfortunately it appeared at the same time as the five-cylinder Honda; as if this was not enough, so too did the four-cylinder Yamaha two-stroke, which Phil Read and Bill Ivy used to such good effect. This meant that the Ducati was outgunned and it was never used in a full-scale World Championship attempt. This is sad, because Taglioni had drawn up the design some years earlier in 1959. If only the Ducati management had authorized him to proceed! Things might then have been very different when Honda launched its bid for World Championship honours in the 125 cc class with its twin-cylinder machines. The Ducati 125 four-cylinder racer on display at the London Earls Court Show staged between 16 and 23 September 1967. The company's prototype 350 Mark 3 'wide-case' production roadster is in the background.

Vic Camp runner Tom Phillips (38) attempts to pass Cyril Howard (Moto Guzzi) in the 350 cc race at the Snetterton, Norfolk 'Race of Aces' meeting July 1967. Phillips' machine is one of a pair (a 250, besides his 350) that Camp provided for him. Compared to the 'racers' he sold to the public, these two bikes were much quicker, with special high-lift cams, titanium connecting rods, and forged slipper pistons. They also used proper racing brakes by Oldani in place of the standard production alloy hubs.

Italian *Classic* Gallery

Factory tester and works rider Bruno Spaggiari with the Bologna factory's 350 Desmo single-cylinder racer, at Cesenatico in 1969. Spaggiari turned in a number of outstanding performances at Italian international meetings during that year on the 350 (and on the 250 and 450 cc versions), including a tremendous race with World Champion Phil Read on a TR2 Yamaha. Specification of the works development Ducati included 42 mm carburettor, dry clutch, special Marzocchi forks and Oldani brakes.

Italian *Classic* Gallery

May 1972: John Blunt, shop manager at Mick Walker motorcycles, sits astride the prototype Walker Ducati racer. From early 1972 until the end of 1973, over 30 of these machines were built, using both narrow- and wide-case Ducati overhead camshaft, single-cylinder engines, in both valve spring and desmodromic form. The first machines used Saxon-built frames. These were later replaced by Spondon frames because of slow deliveries. Most of the bikes were 350s, but there were also some 250s and 450s.

Below: The day that brought the Ducati V-twin instant fame: 23 May 1972, and an amazing 1-2 victory against the cream of the world's superbikes, at the inaugural Imola 200-Mile race. Here Paul Smart (16) leads from team mate Bruno Spaggiari (9). The pair finished in this order. The event was a stunning success. Not only did a record crowd of over 70,000 cram the 5 km (3.1 mile), vineyard-bordered circuit, but the Italian factories were out in force for the first time since 1957. Ducati fielded four works riders – with a choice of 10 factory machines. Moto Guzzi entered three machines, and MV Agusta had two mounts out in practice, although only Giacomo Agostini started the race (team mate Pagani was a non-starter). Besides these there were four works BSA and Triumph threes, three factory Nortons, a pair of works Hondas, and several semi-works machines.

Opposite top: The British Ducati importer (1967-73) was the enthusiastic Vic Camp (with glasses), pictured here with his mechanic Bert Furness. Camp sponsored a number of riders, including Tom Phillips, Paul Smart, Chas Mortimer, Ken Watson and Alan Dunscombe, on a variety of single-cylinder models from the Bologna factory. He also built a considerable number of race-kitted roadsters, like the one illustrated. These offered the club rider an inexpensive mount, but little else, as they were simply roadsters at heart, stripped of lights and other street equipment and fitted with glassfibre ware.

Below: Following the worldwide acclaim arising from its Imola victory, Ducati was inundated with requests for replicas of Paul Smart's bike. The firm responded by producing a limited number of hand-built super sportsters code-named 750 SS. Around 200 of these were ultimately built in 1973 and 1974. These replicas shared the same 80 x 74.4 mm bore and stroke dimensions of the standard production GT and Sport models, which gave a capacity of 747.95 cc (identical to the 1972 Imola machines).

The motorcycle in the photograph is one of 24 imported into Britain in 1974 (none came in during 1973) and belonged to Doug Lunn, who worked as a salesman for the importers Coburn and Hughes. Lunn raced the machine with considerable success on the British short circuits during 1974 and 1975. He also rode it in the Isle of Man TT.

Ducati's next success with the V-twin at international level came at Montjuich Park, Barcelona, in July 1973, when Benjamin Grau and Salvador Canellas won the prestigious 24 Hours endurance race. The machine they used had a capacity of 863.90 cc (86 x 74.4 mm) and was the prototype of a new, larger engine from the Bologna company. The new machine won with a massive 16-lap advantage, tucking 2694.97 km (1674.58 miles) into the 24 hours. The following year Grau and Canellas were back but after 16 hours, and with a 9-lap advantage, they were forced out with gearbox trouble. In 1975 Ducati went all out to take the FIM Coupe d'Endurance Championship. The season could not have started better, with another victory in the Barcelona 24 Hours. This photograph shows Grau (who was again partnered by Canellas) on his way to another highly impressive victory. At the end the pair led by 11 laps, logging a total of 731 laps. This amounted to 2771.61 km (1722.2 miles), a new record.

Mike Hailwood with one of the two machines which the factory built for him to race in the 1978 Isle of Man Formula 1 TT: one for the race, one for practice and as a spare. On this V-twin, entered by the Manchester dealers, Sports Motorcycles, Hailwood went on to create history with a sensational victory over the might of the Japanese Honda team. Honda's top rider, multi-World Champion Phil Read was forced to retire after trying in vain to keep his Honda in front of the Italian V-twin.

One of the special works NCR V-twins built for Hailwood to use in the 1978 TT. The machines were based around the standard production 900SS of the period, but with a lot of special components and much additional tuning and attention to detail. The engine retained the original 846 cc (86 x 74.4 mm) capacity, and produced around 88 bhp at 9000 rpm.

Although the original 900SS 40 mm pumper Dell'Ortos were retained, the heads were specially gas-flowed and ported. In addition there were larger valves – the inlet going up to 43 mm (39 mm) and the exhaust to 39 mm (36 mm), together with an increase to 11:1 compression, for the one-off forged, three-ring pistons.

Combined with a vast amount of lightening of the internal parts of the engine, these changes gave more usable power at lower engine revolutions. The standard ignition system was discarded in favour of a Lucas Rita transistorized one. An air-cooled clutch was the most obvious difference in the transmission, but the gearbox had also been modified, with dogs removed from fourth gear to give a slicker shift.

Garelli

One of the two 1963 record-breaking Garelli machines without its fairing. Prepared under the direction of Ing. Soncini, the factory's development chief, the two machines were identical, powered by conventional piston port engines with 40 x 39 mm bore and stroke dimensions. Normal primary gear drive, multi-plate clutches and four-speed gearboxes with twistgrip-operated change were used. It was also intended to have standard flywheel magneto ignition. However, after this had shown symptoms of trouble during preliminary tests, it was replaced by battery and coil with the contact breaker mounted on the crankshaft end, giving a fixed advance of only 14 degrees.

The records broken by these Garellis included the six-hours, at 122.15 km/h (75.95 mph), the 1000 km at 116.36 km/h (72.35 mph), and the all-important 24 hours at 108.71 km/h (67.50 mph) – a speed that was also sufficient to break the 75 cc, 100 cc, and even the 125 cc records for this category.

The team of technicians, led by Ing. William Soncini, and the six riders (Marchesani, Pastoni, Patrignani, Pernigotti, Spinello and Zubani) with one of the two fully faired Garellis that broke a number of world records in the 50 and 75 cc classes on 3 and 4 November 1963. The record attempts, which took place in atrocious weather conditions, were staged at Monza Autodrome, near Milan.

The supremely neat Veglia Garelli special built in late 1976. It employed disc valve induction and a German Kreidler top end. This Garelli was competitive enough to finish the 1977 season well up in the Italian Senior Championship. Sponsorship came from Veglia, the famous instruments manufacturer.

Engine of the 49 cc Garelli which, ridden by George Ashton, took the British 50 cc championship in the late 1960s. It produced between 13 and 14 bhp and successfully outpaced the previously all-conquering Honda CR 110s, which had dominated the championships for several years. It was similar to the earlier Garelli record breaker.

The 1982 World Championship-winning 125 Garelli twin was based around the successful Minarelli design. This bike, ridden by Angel Nieto and Eugenio Lazzarini, had a 124.62 cc (44.41 mm) disc valve engine that provided a class-beating 46.8 bhp at 14,600 rpm. The gearbox was a six-speeder and the dry weight was 77.5 kg (170.9 lb).

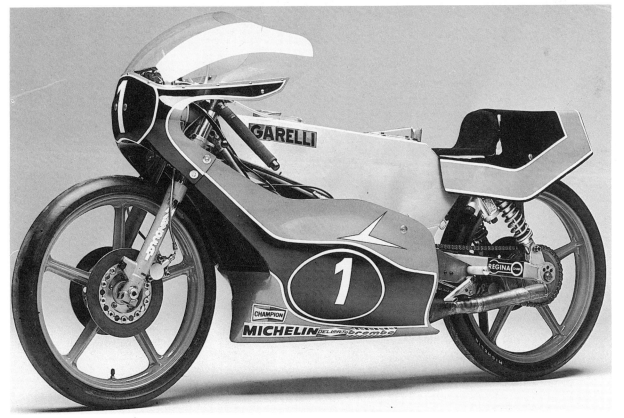

Main picture: Start of the **1983 125 cc** West German Grand Prix at Hockenheim. The Garelli pair of Nieto (1) and Lazzarini (2) are furthest from the camera on the front row of the grid. They finished in this order. At the end of the season Nieto had retained his grip on the World title, with Lazzarini third.

Inset: The **1983 125 cc** World Champion, the Spaniard Angel Nieto with his super-fast Garelli twin during the Italian Grand Prix at Monza that year. He won at record speed.

Gilera

Gilera first hit the headlines in 1937 when Piero Taruffi broke the 1 hour record at a speed of 195.26 km/h (121.33 mph) riding a fully enclosed, water-cooled, four-cylinder machine developed from the earlier Rondine. This basic design was steadily improved through an intensive racing programme, and in 1939 Gilera was well on the way to achieving supremacy in the 500 cc class. Twice during the season Serafini achieved magnificent victories – beating BMW on its own ground in the German Grand Prix and winning the Ulster Grand Prix at record speed.

When racing began again after the Second World War, Gilera returned with air-cooled, four-cylinder machines. At first their speed advantage was offset by poor handling and lack of low speed torque, but patient development overcame the problems. Gilera's first World Championship came in 1950 when Umberto Masetti took the title. From then on success followed success, until the Arcore company withdrew from racing at the

end of 1957. In the eight years from 1950 Gilera riders Masetti, Duke and Liberati achieved the 500 cc Championship six times, winning 31 Classic events in the process. It was on a Gilera, too, that Bob McIntyre scored a Junior and Senior TT double, and became the first rider to lap the Isle of Man Mountain circuit at over 160 km/h (100 mph). In addition there have been the performances of the sidecar star Ercole Frigero, consistently brilliant but sometimes rather overlooked. For several years he was second only to the great Eric Oliver in the Sidecar World Championship.

When Gilera retired from the sport it did so on the crest of a magnificent wave, in a series of record breaking ventures at Monza.

Although Gilera made a number of comebacks during the next decade, notably with the Scuderia Duke team in 1963 and the Argentinian star Caldarella the following year, the company was never able to recapture its former glory.

World Championships: 500 cc 1950, 1952, 1953, 1954, 1955 and 1957

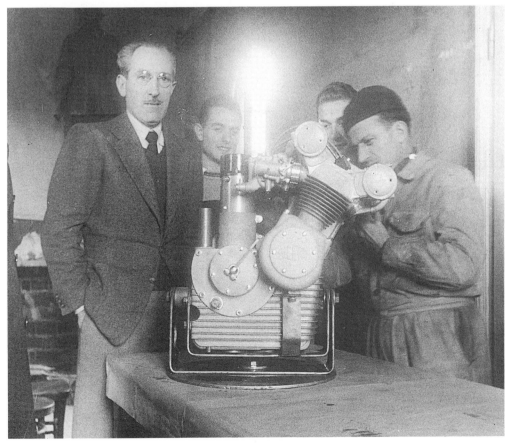

Above: Another view of the 1948 version of the Gilera multi-cylinder engine. In its original form it had a serious lubrication problem, which was not really solved until after Remor had left Gilera. There are people close to the Gilera factory who state that Remor, although academically brilliant, was rather lacking in practical skills – and a somewhat difficult person. Nello Pagani for one found this to be the case.

Left: The 1948 version of the Gilera Saturno San Remo racer. Introduced the previous year, this version had been developed from the original pre-Second World War design by Ing. Salmaggi. The 498.76 cc (84 x 90 mm) long-stroke overhead valve engine produced 35 bhp at a lowly 6000 rpm. It was to remain unchanged until 1951, when an improved version appeared with updated suspension.

Right: Ing. Piero Remor (*left*) and other members of the firm's race shop in the spring of 1948, with the new unblown Gilera 496.692 cc (52 x 58 mm) four-cylinder engine for which he was largely responsible. In late 1949 Remor left to join the rival MV Agusta, where he was responsible for the design of a very similar engine.

Above: The great Scottish rider Fergus Anderson tries the position of the Gilera Saturno on which Artesiani had just won the 500 cc class of the 1948 Italian GP at Faenza. 'Very comfortable' was his verdict. The Faenza circuit was chosen for the event as the Monza Autodrome was still out of use following extensive war damage.

Carlo Bandirola with the 1949 version of the four-cylinder Gilera. This differed from the following year's version in its brake (it had a full-width type in 1950) and the eccentric rear suspension, which was dropped after Remor left the company.

Top left: The Spanish GP 1951. In the 500 cc race the winner Umberto Masetti, on one of two Gilera fours in the event, leads Les Graham's MV Agusta. The MV man had to retire with gear selector troubles.

This was to be Masetti's only classic victory that year; Britain's Geoff Duke took the title the Gilera star had won in 1950.

Top right: Side shot of Masetti's Spanish GP race winner. Note the upright riding position, comprehensive mudguards, and its straight pipes, rather than megaphones. The power output of the 1951 Arcore four was 50 bhp at 9100 rpm.

For 1951 the Gilera designer Ing. Passoni (who had replaced Remor) followed the successful Norton move of the previous year by adopting telescopic forks, a duplex frame and swinging arm rear suspension. This revised model appeared at the inaugural Spanish GP. Staged in early April over the twists and turns of Montjuich Park, Barcelona, there were two of the 'new' Gilera fours taking part. One was ridden by Nello Pagani, who is shown here sitting on the machine, watched by team manager Piero Taruffi.

Opposite: Gilera new boy Libero Liberati receiving attention in his pit at the Italian Grand Prix in September 1951. He finished the race in 7th place. The other members of the team – Milani, Masetti and Pagani – finished 1st, 2nd and 3rd respectively. Later Liberati became the company's final 500 cc World Champion – in 1957, the year Gilera, together with Moto Guzzi and Mondial, withdrew from the sport.

The first public appearance of the double-knocker Saturno Bialbero Corsa came during practice for the 1952 Italian GP at Monza. It was also used that year in the Spanish GP in October. Even though it produced 45 bhp at 8000 rpm, it was not developed further because of the success gained by its more exotic four-cylinder brothers. It shared its bore and stroke dimensions with the production overhead valve Saturno model. The engine was the work of Ing. Franco Passoni.

Ernesto Soprani keeps his Saturno single ahead of a factory four-cylinder model in the 1953 Spanish Grand Prix held at Montjuich Park, Barcelona. The race was won by Fergus Anderson on a works Moto Guzzi.

In 1953 Geoff Duke and Reg Armstrong joined Gilera. Both were former members of the British Norton team. They brought not only their riding talent, but their experience; both were to prove vital for the future development of the Arcore four-cylinder racers.

Amongst the features tried that year was a smaller wheel (17 in rim at the rear) with a 4.00 section tyre. This, it will be noted, was something Norton had also experimented with. The tank, seat and flyscreen also looked very Norton-like.

Over 100,000 spectators witnessed the Swedish Grand Prix held on 17 and 18 July 1954. In the 500 cc race, Reg Armstrong on a Gilera set the fastest lap at 164.99 km/h (102.52 mph), but dropped back to finish 3rd after refuelling on the 27th lap of the 209.99 km (130.48 mile) race.

Long-stroke, wet clutch 246 cc Aermacchi belonging to Pete Ownsworth at Snetterton, August 1962.

Kel Carruthers, the 1969 250 cc World Champion, and Benelli four-cylinder.

Above: Anglo-Italian. The Aermacchi Metisse Italian power unit fitted into British Rickman Brothers chassis. The combination worked well.

Snetterton, September 1964. Mechanic about to push-start John Blanchard's 250 Aermacchi into life.

'Mike the Bike' Hailwood in action during the 1963 Senior TT on his MV Agusta 'fire engine'.

Linto 500. The work of Ing. Lino Tonti, this was essentially a pair of Aermacchi 250 Ala d'Oro racing engines in a common crankcase. It proved fast, but not totally reliable (Alan Cathcart).

Italian *Classic* Gallery

Main picture: Terry Grotefeld brought his immaculate green and white Aermacchi home 3rd in the 1964 Lightweight event, the first 250 cc Manx GP since 1947.

Inset: Tom Jackson with a 246 cc Aermacchi Ala d'Oro at Snetterton, 1964.

Below: The Baines brothers, Geoff and John, with their 888 cc bevel-driven Ducati V-twin. It started life as a 1974 750 cc SS Desmo.

Main picture: Tony Rutter won four World TT Formula 2 Championship titles on works Ducatis during the early 1980s. The engine was a tuned version of the production Pantah unit.

Top left: Swedish rider Ulf Svensson raced this pair of ex-works, double-knocker Ducatis throughout Europe during 1961 and 1962. Photograph taken at International Cadwell Park, September 1962.

Top right: World Champion Phil Read (MV) in race-winning form at Scarborough, September 1974.

Garelli's water-cooled 125 cc parallel twin engine, good for almost 50 bhp and over 225 km/h (140 mph)! It was the last Italian bike to win a World title the 1984 125 cc Championship.

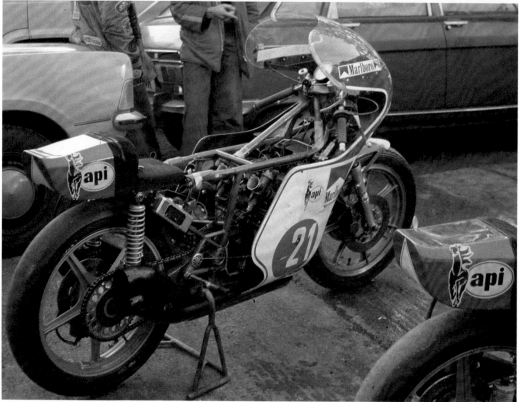

Final outing for Agostini on an MV Agusta was when he rode this 350 four at Brands Hatch in October 1976.

Engine unit of the fabulous V6
Laverda. It was the joint work of
former Maserati engineer Giulio Alfieri
and Laverda's chief designer Luciano
Zen.

Ing. Taglioni and Franco Farné, the
men behind Ducati's success on road
and track.

89

Italian *Classic* Gallery

Works Ducati Pantah 600 Formula 2 racer pictured in the Bologna factory, with roadster 500 SLs in the background.

MV Agusta 500 three-cylinder. Ridden by Giacomo Agostini it was destined to become the most successful Grand Prix racer in the Blue Riband category during the late 1960s and early 1970s.

Works FB Mondial of the type used by the factory to win the 1957 250 cc World Championship, ridden by Cecil Sandford.

V6 Laverda pictured during the 1978 Bol d'Or race. Riders Cereghini and Perugini were forced to retire with a broken universal joint. Before this the bike had been timed at almost 290 km/h (180 mph) – over 30 km/h faster than the winning works Honda.

Main picture: Bill Lomas in action on the fully streamlined 500 Moto Guzzi V-8. It is widely held that this was the most fabulous racing motorcycle of all time.

Above: Roadster-based 750 MV four, as used by Agostini in the 1972 Imola 200 race. This is a later shot, after it had been converted to chain final drive.

Right: In 1979-80 Laverda built batches of the 500 Formula racer for use in Italian Junior events. It was based on the Alpino dohc roadster twin.

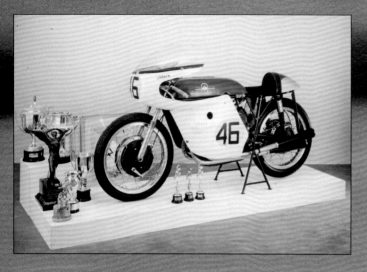

Main picture: Englishman Arthur Wheeler campaigned with Moto Guzzis for a decade between 1952 and 1962. He is shown here on the Reynolds-framed version on which he finished 3rd in the 1962 World Championship series.

Above: Gilera 500 four-cylinder racer. It was raced in this guise by Minter, Hartle and Read during the Scuderia Duke era, c. 1963.

Above right: Giuseppe Pattoni produced a variety of dohc twins with 250, 350 and 500 cc engine sizes. An example of the largest is pictured here. It is one of the machines originally built for Liverpool sponsor Bill Hannah and raced by Billie Nelson and Fred Stevens in the early 1970s.

Italian *Classic* Gallery

Factory-built Ducati outside the Bologna works, January 1979. On the left is a 500 cc Pantah, on the right a 900 V-twin.

Superbly prepared 125 cc Aspes two-stroke single cylinder club racer on display at the Milan Show, November 1977.

On 14 October 1954, Piero Taruffi piloted this strange-looking 'double torpedo-shaped' device called the Tarf. By then Taruffi was competition director of the Gilera company at Arcore. His record-breaking spree (he netted a total of some 20, up to the 200 km distance) was achieved at the banked Montlhéry circuit, near Paris. The Tarf was powered by one of the works four-cylinder 500 engines.

Libero Liberati winning the first round of the Senior Italian Championships, 19 March 1955. This was the first year that Gilera used the full 'dustbin' alloy streamlined shell. Note the large side vent to allow cooling air to reach the cylinders. The meeting was staged over the Naples circuit (Circuito di Napoli).

Gilera

The Gileras of Alfredo Milani (40) and Giuseppe Colnago (38) lead the Moto Guzzi rider Ken Kavanagh (4) on the Circuito di Senigallia, 31 July 1955. Victory in this Italian event went to Milani after a close-fought battle. Of the four Milani brothers, Alfredo was the most gifted and stayed with Gilera throughout his racing career.

Ireland's Reg Armstrong rounds the Governor's Bridge dip during the Senior TT, 10 June 1955. Armstrong, who chose the 1954 limited streamlining for his mount, finished 2nd to team mate Geoff Duke, at an average speed of 155.69 km/h (96.74 mph) for the seven laps.

Romolo Ferri in action at Monza in the 125 cc race at the Italian GP on Sunday 9 September 1956. After challenging with MV Agusta star Carlo Ubbiali for the lead, the tiny Gilera twin expired with a holed piston. Throughout its career the 124.656 cc (40 x 49.6 mm) engine was troubled with reliability problems. Although fast the machine only ever won a single classic, the 1956 German GP at Solitude. The engine, inclined forwards at 30 degrees, owed much to the larger four-cylinder models. Besides Ferri the other rider of the design was Enzo Vezzalini.

Following the huge success of its 500 cc four-cylinder model, the Gilera factory built a smaller 349.66 cc (46 x 52.6 mm) version. This made a convincing winning début in the classics when ridden by Liberati at Monza on 9 September 1956. The Gilera star won the 27-lap, 155.25 km (96.47 mile) long race at an average speed of 178.39 km/h (110.85 mph). He also set a record fastest lap for the class at 184.82 km/h (114.84 mph).

Above: Reg Armstrong (Gilera), winner of the 500 cc German Grand Prix, held on Sunday 22 July 1956 and run over the superb Solitude circuit near Stuttgart. Armstrong won at an average speed of 148.09 km/h (92.02 mph) from Masetti's MV Agusta. This came after the sensational retirement of Geoff Duke (Gilera), Bill Lomas (Moto Guzzi), and local favourite Walter Zeller (BMW).

Top right: A technical masterpiece exposed to the world. This superb drawing was commissioned by Gilera from the artist Cavara in 1956. It shows what was underneath the comprehensive streamlining of the latest 499.49 cc (52 x 58.8 mm) Arcore 'fire engine' that year.

Right: Geoff Duke displays all the style that made him the most successful rider of the early and mid-1950s during his victorious ride in the 500 cc Italian GP, 9 September 1956. There were an amazing six Gilera fours in the race: Duke's and those of Reg Armstrong, Pierre Monneret, Alfredo Milano, Libero Liberati and Giuseppe Colnago.

336

GILERA 500 4C.

Italian Classic Gallery

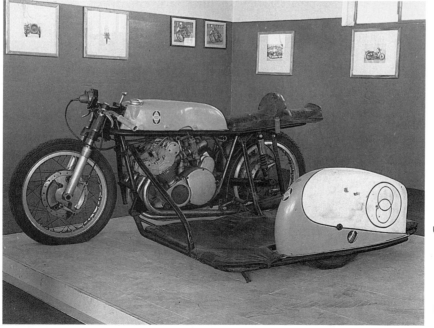

The 1956 Italian Grand Prix Sidecar race winner, Albino Milani. An outstanding speed superiority over the opposition made victory a certainty, barring trouble. The Gilera star went on to win at an average speed of 157.92 km/h (98.13 mph) from Pip Harris (Norton) and a gaggle of German BMWs led by Fritz Hillebrand. The nearest Albino Milani ever got to being Sidecar World Champion came in 1952 when, again on a Gilera, he finished 2nd to the great Englishman, Eric Oliver.

A sidecar outfit, powered by the Gilera 500 four-cylinder, of the type used by Albino Milani to win the class in the Italian GP at Monza in both 1956 and 1957. Included in the specification were four Dell'Orto SS25A racing carburettors, a lowered frame and suspension, a 3.25 x 18 rear and 3.50 x 19 front tyres, with a 4.00 x 12 for the sidecar wheel.

Gilera

Superb action shot of Saturno Corsa rider Giovanni Pio. His Saturno is one of the very last built and displays the attractive lines of the machine to perfection: c. 1957.

The production Saturno Corsa (racing) model was sold between late 1951 and 1957. The final version (illustrated) was first offered in 1956 and was without doubt the most handsome and purposeful of all, with its telescopic forks, swinging arm rear suspension and full-width front brake. The Saturno was also sold in sports, roadster and motocross form, and was thus a contemporary equivalent of the British BSA Gold Star.

Left: Gilera works riders Libero Liberati (*left,* in coat) and Bob McIntyre at Monza Autodrome in 1957 with one of the 'dustbin'-faired Gilera fours. Both riders were to meet with fatal accidents in 1962. Liberati was killed in a road accident near his home town of Terni while riding a Gilera Saturno; McIntyre was fatally injured racing at Oulton Park in August that year on a 500 Norton.

Above right: The Australian Bob Brown was brought in by Gilera for the Golden Jubilee Isle of Man TT races in June 1957. Our photograph shows Brown's machine (76) before the start of the Senior event, in which he finished 3rd at an average speed of 154.19 km/h (95.81 mph). A former Sydney taxi driver, Brown came to Europe in 1955. Right from the start he put in some highly impressive performances on Matchless, AJS and NSU machines. He was a friend of Geoff Duke, and it was the latter's Imola accident that led to his TT ride.

Above far right: Perhaps Gilera's most renowned mechanic of the classic era: the talented Angelo Fumigalli, seen here at the TT in June 1957.

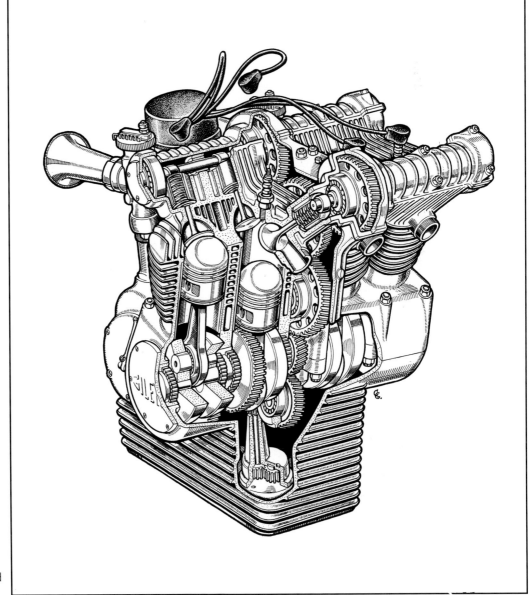

Right: The Gilera engine, showing helical gear drive to the double overhead camshafts, high-dome forged pistons, coil valve springs, centrally mounted sparkplugs, together with gear-type oil pump and massive finned sump.

Italian *Classic* Gallery

Ing. Franco Pasoni (*left*) with one of the 174.8 cc (46 x 52.6 mm) Formula 2 twin racing engines. Derived from the smaller Grand Prix unit, the 175 was intended for events such as the Giro d'Italia. But the combination of Gilera's withdrawal in 1957 and the government's ban on such long-distance road events as the Giro the same year, sealed its fate. This photograph was taken in winter 1962-3 just before the company's return to the sport.

Bottom left: The Gilera race shop gathering dust in late 1962. After five long years away from the circuit, the lack of use is evident from the disorganized remains of what were once the most glamorous machines in the World Championship series. A few short months later this mass of machines and components was to be readied for battle once more.

Bottom right: Duke, Minter and journalist Charlie Rous at Monza in reflective mood. At the beginning hopes were high. However, an accident at Brands Hatch in April 1963 was to sideline Minter for the greater part of the season.

Gilera

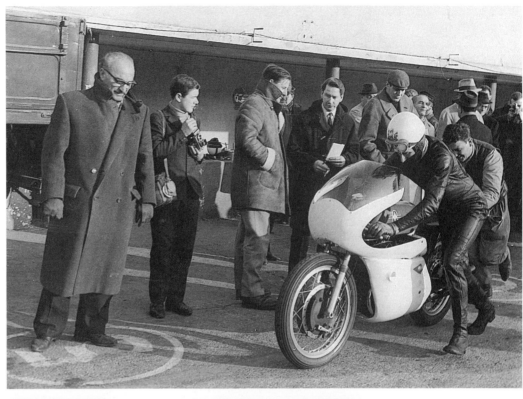

Monza Autodrome, March 1963. The Gilera racing effort is reborn through Scuderia Duke. A group of journalists from around the world wait as John Hartle receives some help as he prepares to start one of the fours.

Duke with the smaller Gilera four at the 1963 Isle of Man TT, with chief mechanic Fumagalli. Rider John Hartle finished 2nd to Jim Redman's Honda four. A good enough performance, but not sufficient to satisfy racing enthusiasts who imagined that the Arcore factory could resume the domination it enjoyed in an earlier era.

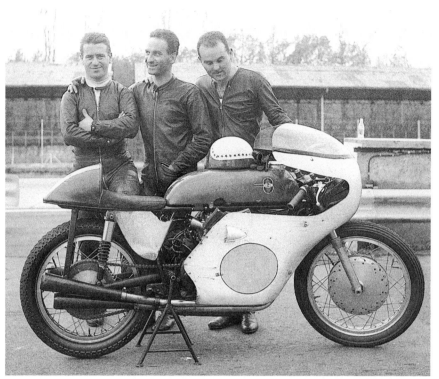

In October 1963 Gilera invited various riders to test the fours at Monza. Included were Milani (Aermacchi), Mancini (Motobi), and Rossi (Bianchi). However, none of these was contracted; instead the Argentine star Benedicto Caldarella appeared on the Arcore four the following year. He began with his historic ride in the 500 cc United States GP at Daytona, where he led Hailwood on the MV Agusta at the beginning of the race.

The arrival of Benedicto Caldarella in Italy on 12 April 1964 was marred by a strike at the Gilera factory in Arcore. It caused the company's planned press conference to be called off. However, this did not stop the Argentinian ace testing a 500 Gilera four at Monza (illustrated). The following Sunday, 22 April, Caldarella stole the show at the international meeting at Imola. There he won the 500 cc race and hoisted the absolute race record to a sizzling 146.87 km/h (91.29 mph) in the process.

The Gilera four's last outing was at Brands Hatch on 9 October 1966; the former Suzuki works star Frank Perris (8), and the Italian veteran Remo Venturi (4), rode a pair of the machines in the Race of the South and the 500 cc Redex Trophy. However, both were destined to finish midfield, among the privateers: a sad ending to a glorious career.

After his victory at Imola, Caldarella (white shirt) chats to Comm. Giuseppe Gilera, then 75 years old. But after his superb start to the season, things did not go to plan. Not only were there a series of crippling strikes at the Gilera works that year, but this also caused the first of the company's financial problems. These were to lead ultimately to the Piaggio takeover in 1969. With money short, Caldarella was not to receive anything other than a token back-up, which consisted of a single mechanic and an old van. Of course this was hardly enough to challenge, let alone defeat, the might of MV Agusta.

Gori

In 1974 and 1975 Guido Valli used this Gori to become Italian Hillclimb Champion. The machine had a 123.6 cc (54 x 54 mm) German Sachs engine. Running on a 13:1 compression ratio it produced 25 bhp at 11,600 rpm and was capable of 185 km/h (115 mph). Other technical details included 34 mm Bing carburettor, six-speed gearbox, Marzocchi suspension, 170 mm Fontana double-sided 2LS front brake, Motoplat electronic ignition and full cradle duplex frame.
A production version was offered for sale to private customers in 1975 and 1976.

Italemmezata

From 1958 until he established the Italjet marque in 1966, Leopoldo Tartarini ran the Italemmezeta company. As well as various roadsters with a variety of power units, MZ among them, Italemmezeta built a 50 cc two-stroke racer in 1965 called the Vampiro ('Vampire'). The machine was also used to publicize the new Italjet name, hence the logo on tank and fairing. Its racing efforts were limited to Italian club and national events, although a stray example retired in the 1965 TT.

Itom

The distinction of being the first woman to ride in an Isle of Man TT went to Londoner Mrs Beryl Swain, in the 1962 50 cc event. Her mount was a race-kitted Itom and she finished the 2-lap race in 22nd position, at an average speed of 77.78 km/h (48.33 mph). She is pictured here in April 1962 at the Brands Hatch circuit in Kent.

Italian *Classic* Gallery

The Itom Competizione 49 cc racer was the result of Anglo-Italian cooperation. The Milanese concern rapidly built a reputation through the 1950s as a producer of quality ultra-lightweight motorcycles up to 65 cc, and of cyclomotors and mopeds, offering speed and reliability. Dick Chalaye, of the London dealers A.H. Tooley, was the man responsible. On offer was a vast range of tuning 'goodies' and glassfibre ware enabling Itom to be converted into a cheap and reliable racer. Early models had a three-speed, twistgrip-operated gear change. Later on came an extra gear, and finally a positive stop foot change.

Lambretta

During 1950 and 1951 Lambretta broke a number of distance and speed records. The engine chosen for this task was a specially prepared version of the firm's 52 x 58 mm 125 cc unit. To ensure that enough power would be available, it was decided to fit a supercharger. This was mounted on the nearside, where the magneto normally went: the magneto was discarded in favour of a simple battery/coil system. The cylinder barrel, piston and head, plus the bottom end, were very similar to the production engine – even the three-speed twistgrip gearbox was retained. The clutch featured an extra plate to cope with the additional power: reputed to be 13.5 bhp at 9000 rpm. The fuel was a special brew with a methanol base, and the exhaust was built to suit the supercharger. However, the frame and streamlining were the biggest innovations.

Besides building a 247 cc, 90°, across the frame overhead camshaft V-twin racer, the famous Lambretta scooter marque also constructed this interesting little 123 cc (52 x 58 mm), single-cylinder two-stroke. Known as the 2t, it appeared in 1949 and featured a conventional piston port induction cylinder and four-speed gearbox. More unusual features included a pivoting-fork rear suspension with a torsion bar parallel to the pivot bearing, and shaft final drive through the offside tube of the fork. The torsion bar was situated a few inches below the pivot and was connected to the fork by a parallelogram linkage.

Most magnificent of all the record attempts by Lambretta was the last. For this the Milanese factory chose Romolo Ferri, who is seen here being congratulated by Herr Frankenburg of NSU (whose company built Lambretta scooters under licence from 1951 to 1956) after Ferri had smashed five world records on 10 August 1951. The venue chosen for this was a section of the Munich-Ingolstadt Autobahn in West Germany and results included covering the flying start kilometre in 17.95 sec, a speed equal to 201 km/h (125 mph). Earlier Ferri had been part of the three-man team (the others were Ambrosini and Rizzi) who on 5 October 1950 at Montlhéry shattered the 1000 km, 6 hours and 12 hours records with speeds of 132.51 km/h (82.34 mph), 132.92 km/h (82.59 mph) and 132.51 km/h (82.35 mph) respectively.

Although Lambretta did not let its racing motorcycles get beyond the prototype stage, it did build and sell a genuine racing scooter. This was raced in Italy and, like the one shown here in Australia in 1953, abroad with considerable success. Strangely, its biggest challenge came from a similar machine constructed by MV Agusta.

Laverda

The first Laverda motorcycle was a 75 cc model which appeared in 1948. The success of this venture led the Breganze company to prepare a machine for the 1951 Milan-Taranto event. In fact it had to retire, but even so factory chief Francesco Laverda had been impressed enough by what he had seen to try again the following year.

By 1953 the marque was the dominant force in the 75 cc category of the long-distance races held in Italy at that time, with Laverda taking the first 14 places in the class at the Milan-Taranto classic!

For 1954 the 75 cc engine was increased to 100 cc. It was just as successful as the smaller unit in long-distance racing events. The exact capacity was 98 cc (52 x 42 mm) and the machine was equipped with an extremely neat, full-cradle duplex frame, telescopic forks and swinging arm rear suspension.

Right: In the early 1970s Laverda made a return to racing with its new 750 SFC twin. This employed a 743.9 cc chain-driven, overhead camshaft vertical twin engine, developed from the earlier 654 cc model that had first appeared back in 1966. The first SFC had drum brakes, but by 1974 – the year of the model shown here – it had gained triple discs. The 1974 model still retained points ignition, which was replaced by an electronic set-up the following year.
The success of the SFC (and its touring stablemate, the SF) was instrumental in establishing the marque in the all-important export markets around the world.

Far right: Pete (P.K.) Davies keeps his Laverda Jota in front of Bill Mark's Fran Ridewood-sponsored Norton Commando at Thruxton in the summer of 1976. Davies' mount was by far the quickest bike in production sports machine racing that year. *Motor Cycle* had timed the Jota at a mean 221.77 km/h (137.8 mph) at MIRA, with a fastest one-way speed of 225.37 km/h (140.04 mph). This was the fastest speed up to then by a production motorcycle in any published road test.
In racing, the Jota's power was proved when Davies won the Avon Series.

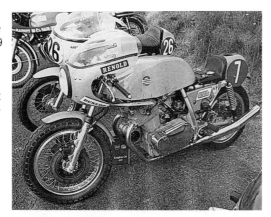

Roger Slater, the British Laverda importer, 1970-81, did much to create a special aura around the make. His enthusiasm for the marque rubbed off on others. One of his leading dealers, Mead and Tomkinson, entered this 1000 cc three-cylinder model in the Liège 24-hour endurance race in 1974. The photograph shows the machine receiving some intensive work in the pit area during the race.

Laverda V6 engine. The specification included 1,000 cc with double overhead camshafts and water cooling. Six downdraught carburettors were fitted into the 'V' and the exhausts on each side merged into a single pipe. An ignition distributor was located vertically at the front and oil was carried in the large-capacity sump. The gearbox was built in unit, and shaft final drive was employed. With such a massive engine there was very little frame – what there was being of the spine variety, with the engine assembly slung below it and braced with subsidiary tubing.

The awesome Laverda V6. This was
constructed over a two-year period in
1976 and 1977. It was the combined
work of Laverda chief designer Lucian
Zen and former Maserati car engineer
Giulio Alfieri. It made its public bow
at the Milan Show in November 1977.
Although great things were expected
from this glamorous bike, it was only
raced once, at the French Bol d'Or in
1978. Ridden by the pairing of
Cereghini and Perugini, it was retired
after 8.5 hours with a broken universal joint. Before this it had been
timed at almost 290 km/h (180 mph)
– by far the quickest machine in the
race.

The British Laverda importer Roger
Slater testing one of the Formula 500
Laverda racers at the factory during a
visit in 1979. The Formula 500 was
developed from the Alpino touring
model. A series of races for these
machines was successfully organized
during the late 1970s and carried
through into the early 1980s. Performance was similar to a well prepared
350cc Yamaha LC.

117

Italian *Classic* Gallery

Left: The Swiss-Hungarian Gyula Marsovszky (81) keeps his Italian Linto ahead of Australian Tony Dennehy's Honda (83) during the 500 cc Yugoslav Grand Prix at Opatija, on 14 September 1969. Both machines were twins, developed to succeed the ageing British singles. In the race both retired. Even so when the Linto kept going it recorded some excellent results in Marsovszky's hands that year – borne out by his 2nd place in the World Championships behind Agostini.

Above: Alberto Pagani before the start of the 1969 Senior TT with his works Linto twin. Sitting astride the bike is his father Nello, the first man to win the 125 cc world title aboard a Mondial in 1949. Pagani Junior won the Italian GP at Monza later that year to give Linto its only Grand Prix victory.

Pagani in action during the 1969 Senior TT. After an opening lap of 156.70 km/h (97.37 mph) on his Linto the Italian was forced out on the next circuit in a race dominated by Agostini's factory MV Agusta, with speeds of 168.55 km/h (104.73 mph), the race average and 170.99 km/h (106.25 mph), the fastest lap. As proof of just how dominant the multi-cylinder MV was in those days, 2nd man, Alan Barnett (Kirby Metisse G50), averaged 158.17 km/h (98.28 mph).

Marsovszky again, this time leading a pack of riders headed by the Swede Bo Granath (Husqvarna) during the 500 cc Dutch TT on 26 June 1971. By now the Suzuki and Kawasaki two-stroke had appeared on the scene and Marsovszky was unable to repeat his success of earlier years with the Linto four-stroke twin.

Malanca

In the early 1970s the small Bologna factory of Malanca achieved some fantastic results in the 125 cc World Championship series – thanks to its extremely competitive twin-cylinder water-cooled machine, ridden by Otello Buscherini and designed by Ing. Librenti. The best year was 1974, when the team finished the season in 4th place in the championships.

The photograph shows Buscherini (3) at the start of the Italian GP that year. Also in the frame are Derbi rider Angel Nieto (2), who finished in 3rd place, and the 1974 125 cc champion Kent Anderson (4) with his Yamaha.

Prototype MBA 250 cc racer seen at the British Grand Prix at Silverstone, August 1979. The engine had a bore and stroke of 55 x 52 mm, to give a capacity of 247.08 cc. With disc valve induction, maximum power was 60 bhp at 11,800 rpm. The cylinders were inclined 30° from the vertical. Although never as popular or competitive as the smaller MBA twin, this model was none the less a Grand Prix winner in the hands of the Swiss rider Raymond Freymond, who won the Swedish round at Anderstorp in 1982. He finished 3rd in the World Championships that same year. MBA stands for Morbidelli – Benelli Armi.

MBA had so many problems with the original 250 twin in 1979, that it was forced to recruit the gifted engineers Mar Schouten and Jörg Möller from Holland. The pair are seen here studying the chassis of the machine at the factory.

Above: The original crankshaft (*top*) on the MBA 250 cc caused many problems. When the Dutch engineer Jörg Möller was brought in, he redesigned the engine for the 1980 season, including a new crankshaft (*bottom*).

Top right: The front of MBA factory at San Angelo di Vado, c. 1981. From this small plant came the 1978 and 1980 125 cc World Championship-winning machines ridden by Eugenio Lazzarini and Pier-Paolo Bianchi respectively.

The Czech Grand Prix 1980. The 1980 125 cc World Champion Pier-Paolo Bianchi leads the race on his MBA from Massimiani (Minarelli), Bertain (Motobécane), Müller (MBA), Nieto (Minarelli) and Kneubühler (MBA). At the end of the race the order was Bertain, Massimiani, Müller, Kneübuhler and Bianchi.
The MBA 124.68 cc (44 x 41 mm) engine that year turned out 44 bhp at 14,200 rpm and gave a maximum speed of 220 km/h (137 mph).

121

Italian *Classic* Gallery

The MBA 125 cc 'production' racer assembly line with the covered engines on the left and the chassis on the right. Until the FIM changed the rules in the late 1980s to outlaw twins, these bikes largely dominated the class of all levels of the sport, both in Italy and abroad.

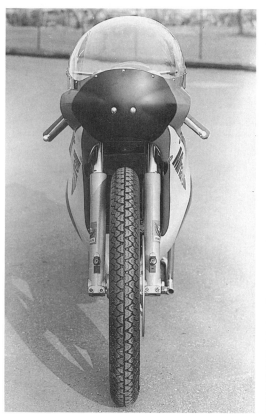

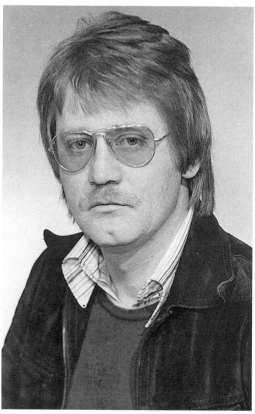

Minarelli

Far left: Frontal view of the Minarelli bicylindrico (twin-cylinder) 125 GP racer.

Left: The brilliant Dutch engineer Jörg Möller was responsible for the design of both the 50 and 125 cc Minarelli racers. At the end of 1981 Minarelli withdrew from the sport and the machines (with a new coat of paint and minor changes) became Garellis.

Minarelli

The Möller-designed 125 Minarelli twin engine, as it appeared in 1980.

Loris Reggiani (who later made a big impact with Aprilia in the 250 cc category) finished a creditable 2nd to team mate Angel Nieto in the 1981 125 cc World Championships. This included a victory on home soil at the San Marino GP, Imola (shown here).

The 1980 and 1981 125 cc World Championship Minarelli team of Angel Nieto (3) and support rider Loris Reggiani (6). By 1981 the Jörg Möller-designed 124.68 cc (44 x 41 mm) engine was giving 45 bhp and could propel the 78 kg (172 lb) machine at over 225 km/h (140 mph).

Mondial

Mondial can truthfully claim to have been largely responsible for a major transformation in the racing world. In 1949, when the 125 cc class was generally regarded with an air of rather superior amusement, Mondial's designer Ing. Alfonso Drusiani produced superbly made double-knocker single-cylinder machines that not only totally overwhelmed the two-stroke opposition in their class, but were actually faster than many of the existing 250, and even 350 cc, bikes!

From then on the 125 cc category constantly increased in stature, to a point where it is a vital focus of attention today, both on the race circuit and the public highway.

For three years running, from 1949 to 1951, Mondial machines and riders won the 125 cc Manufacturer's and Individual World Championships before yielding top honours to MV Agusta and NSU. By 1956, however, Drusiani – who had left the company and subsequently returned – had produced new 125 and 250 cc machines that were destined to be as outstanding as his original design. Unfortunately, their

run of success was also the Mondial swansong. For although in 1957 the Milan company's beautifully streamlined machines won the 125 and 250 cc World Championships, ridden by Tarquinio Provini and Cecil Sandford respectively, Mondial joined Gilera and Moto Guzzi in announcing its retirement from racing at the end of the season.

After this, the Mondial name was maintained for racing enthusiasts to enjoy first by Mike Hailwood 1959 and 1960 on an ex-works 250; then later, in the early 1960s, by the Villa brothers with new two-stroke models.

World Championships: 125 cc 1949, 1950, 1951 and 1957; 250 cc 1957

Right: The fabulous double-knocker 123.5 cc (53 x 56 mm) Mondial engine. It dominated its class from 1948 to the end of 1951, before first MV Agusta and then the German NSU marque took over.

Producing some 12 bhp at 9000 rpm, it was capable of over 128 km/h (80 mph), considerably more than its two-stroke rivals, such as MV, Morini and Montesa. It was designed by Alfonso Drusiani.

Mondial

The machine used by Nello Pagani to secure the very first 125 cc World Championship: the 1949 FB (Frattelli Boselli) Mondial. Displacing 123.5 cc (53 x 56 mm), this was a double-knocker employing shaft and bevel gears to drive its overhead camshafts. In the three-round series, Pagani won in Switzerland and Holland, and scored a 5th in front of his home crowd at Monza.

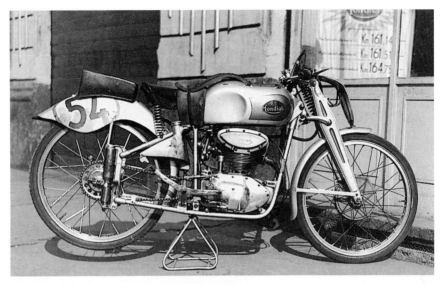

Italian *Classic* Gallery

Above: During practice for the 1949 Italian GP, Mondial works rider Leoni tried this extensively streamlined machine in the 125 cc class. Although not used in the race itself, which Leoni won at an average speed of 125.4 km/h (77.9 mph), it was interesting as an early attempt at comprehensive enclosure. This was a trend that would build up during the early to mid-1950s, until banned by the FIM at the end of the 1957 season.

Inset: The first of the rounds to count towards the World Championships for the 1951 season was held at Barcelona. This was also the very first Spanish Grand Prix, and the 125 cc race went to Guido Leoni on a Mondial with an average speed of 86.20 km/h (53.56 mph). The photograph shows Leoni receiving the victor's laurels from General Moscardo.

Mondial works rider Carlo Ubbiali pushes his machine into life at the start of the 1951 Ultra-Lightweight (125 cc) TT. Although smoking badly, this did not seem to deter its performance as Ubbiali finished 2nd to team mate Cromie McCandless. Even though he won only a single event, Ubbiali in fact scored enough points to become World Champion.
Carlo Ubbiali (born 24 September 1923) went on to win a total of nine World Championships before he retired from the sport at the end of 1960 to concentrate on a business venture.

Italian *Classic* Gallery

Left: In the Grand Prix des Nations at Monza, 9 September 1951, Romolo Ferri gets down to it on his factory Mondial in the 125 cc race. This was Ferri's first ride for the marque, and he repaid Count Boselli by being an excellent runner-up to race winner, and World Champion, Carlo Ubbiali.

Above: Cromie McCandless (*left*), the winner of the 1951 125 cc TT, shakes hands with 2nd place man Carlo Ubbiali. Both rode factory double overhead camshaft FB Mondial – as did the 3rd and 4th riders in, Leoni and Pagani respectively.

The highly complex and overweight double overhead camshaft 250 Mondial twin. Designed by Alfonso Drusiani, it was essentially a pair of the earlier 123.5 cc double-knocker singles in a common crankcase. Although it turned out a highly impressive 35 bhp – almost the equal of the all-conquering NSU Rennmax of the period – the Mondial was fated to achieve nothing of any significance. It was held back by technical problems and too much weight.

Mondial

The English rider Cecil Sandford – destined to be World Champion on a Mondial the following year – after winning the 250 cc class in the Hutchinson 100 meeting at Silverstone, 22 September 1956. He also dominated the 125 cc event, on another Mondial.

Below: Superbly crafted double overhead camshaft 249.1 cc (75 x 56.4 mm), short-stroke FB Mondial engine. Raced in 1956 and 1957, this gave 29 bhp at 10,800 rpm. The rider had a choice of specifying five, six or even seven speeds. Fitted with full streamlining at both front and rear, the 250 Mondial GP was capable of over 215 km/h (135 mph). It was particularly successful in 1957, when it was raced by Tarquinio Provini and Cecil Sandford.

Italian *Classic* Gallery

Mondial pulled out of motorcycle sport at the end of the 1957 season – otherwise this desmodromic 125 single would have continued to feature in the Milan company's racing programme. This photograph was taken in the Mondial pits in that last season, during practice for the 1957 Grand Prix des Nations at Monza.

At the end of 1963 Mondial decided to return to racing, but this time through the talented rider and engineer Francesco Villa. Villa built a 125 single. Raced in 1964 this produced 24 bhp at 11,000 rpm – and against its older Italian four-stroke rivals proved very competitive. However, it was outpaced at Monza that year by the latest Japanese machinery. The photograph shows Francesco Villa astride the seven-speed single in a test session at Modena in March that year.

Late in 1965, at the Italian Championship meeting at Sanremo, Mondial introduced a wholly new 250 twin. With a capacity of 247.3 cc (54 x 54 mm), the newcomer was both air- and water-cooled: air for the heads, water for the cylinders. Like a similar 125 twin that appeared the following year, it featured rotary valve induction and an eight-speed gearbox. Power output was 35 bhp at 9800 rpm, which offered a performance better than 225 km/h (140 mph). Unfortunately, early into the 1966 season Mondial hit financial troubles, which forced the cancellation of its racing programme. Francesco Villa then took the 250 twin to the Spanish Montesa factory, where it was well received. It was used with considerable success over the next couple of years. Meanwhile, Walter Villa went back to the earlier single-cylinder RS Mondial and on a private basis won the Italian Senior 125 cc Championship in both 1966 and 1967.

Morbidelli

The very first Morbidelli racing motorcycle was a 60 cc machine constructed in 1968 for national racing in the Cadet class. There was nothing particularly exciting about its specification, but even so it was responsible for future World Champion Enzo Larrarini winning some of his first races at Castiglione del Lago and Riccione. These successes were instrumental in encouraging industrialist Giancarlo Morbidelli, who had been largely responsible for the machine's construction, to make a more serious commitment to his interest in racing motorcycles. Morbidelli, who owned a large woodworking machinery factory in Pesaro, decided to commission the racer and engineer Franco Ringhini for this purpose.

The first result of this development was the Morbidelli 50 Grand Prix of 1969. Ringhini built this to the latest FIM rules for the class. In other words it featured six speeds and a single cylinder.

Next came a 125 cc twin, with which Gilberto Parlotti gained many victories before losing his

life on the machine during the 1972 TT.

However, the work put in by Ringhini and Parlotti was not wasted, and updated versions of this basic bike scored many important victories throughout the 1970s, including five World Championships. Less successful were the 350 and 500 cc narrow-angle V-fours, which although extremely fast, were far from reliable.

World Championships: 125 cc 1975, 1976, 1977, 1978 and 1980; 250 cc 1977

Italian *Classic* Gallery

The first racing Morbidelli was a 60 cc two-stroke single, which was ridden by the young Enzo Lazzarini to victories at Castiglione del Lago and Riccione in the late 1960s. This encouraged industrialist Giancarlo Morbidelli to hire racer and engineer Franco Ringhini, and a section of Morbidelli's woodwork machinery plant in Pesaro was set aside for the construction of motorcycles. Besides a 50 cc, and eventually a four-cylinder 350, Morbidelli built a number of twin-cylinder 125s both for factory riders and for sale to private customers. One of the latter machines is shown here in 1976.

In 1972 Franco Ringhini designed a 350cc four-cylinder, two-stroke engine with transverse in-line cylinders that were horizontal to the ground. Two rotating discs and vertical carburettors provided the feed. A feature of the bike was its super-light chassis. Morbidelli then hit legal problems, however, as Jawa had already patented a similar engine. Ringhini therefore redesigned the unit. It now had two independent crankshafts and a countershaft with the water pump for the cooling system. Although when tested in 1973 it produced an amazing 95 bhp at 14,000 rpm on the dyno, which was over 25 bhp more than any other GP engine in the class at the time, it soon became clear that vibration was a big problem. This was eventually solved by lowering the power output to 65 bhp. It was not until 1976 that all the problems were sorted out. The West German star Dieter Braun rode the bike that year. His best placing was a 2nd behind the Harley-Davidson of Walter Villa in the Finnish Grand Prix at Imatra.

Morbidelli

During 1977 and 1978 Morbidelli continued to race its narrow-angle 350 V-four, but reliability was a continuing problem. Riders Pileri and Lega were usually well up with the leaders in events but almost invariably the bikes did not last the pace – although Lega did finish 2nd in the 1977 Italian Grand Prix at Imola. For 1979 a 500 cc version was built. This was ridden by Rossi, but its only finish that year was a 9th at Imola. Although the machine promised great things, this was to prove its only placing in the first ten of a World Championship race.

Morini

Originally the co-owner of the MM company, Alfonso Morini broke away to found his own concern in 1937. However, it was not until after the Second World War that he was to establish the new marque in the two-wheel sector.

The first racing machine was a simple, piston port, single-cylinder two-stroke, which was introduced in 1947. In the hands of riders such as Umberto Masetti and Nello Pagani the little Morini soon built up quite a reputation for its speed and reliability. Its main rival in those early postwar days was the very similar MV Agusta 'stroker.

Then the appearance of the entirely new dohc Mondial four-stroke set the two-stroke brigade back on their heels. The result was that after Mondial had soundly beaten both Morini and MV during the first World Championship series in 1949, the two-stroke marques were forced into building their own four-stroke models.

Although of sound design, the Morini, however, was never quite good enough to mount an effective challenge to, first, the Mondial, and later to the MV and NSU. In consequence Morini withdrew from racing at the end of 1952.

During the mid-1950s the success in sports machine racing of its 175 Settebello ohv and Rebello ohc singles put the Bologna marque back in the limelight, and with it Comm. Morini's enthusiasm for having another crack at the Classics.

First an enlarged Rebello was built, which appeared briefly at the end of 1957. However, the real impact of Morini's most famous racing motorcycle – the *Gran Premio* ('Grand Prix') – came at Monza, where Emilio Mendogni and Giampiero Zubani soundly trounced the mighty MV team headed by Carlo Ubbiali, who had just won yet another World title.

Unfortunately, this great victory was not followed up and from 1959 until 1961 the Morini 250 was rather sidelined while others competed. Tarquinio Provini rode it a few times outside Italy, but there were no real results.

Then from 1962 things changed markedly and at last the Provini/Morini combination began to bring in the results.

Without doubt 1963 was the factory's greatest season, with Provini hounding the powerful Japanese Honda Team – and winning as many

Italian *Classic* Gallery

races as he lost. With victories in Spain, West Germany, Italy and the Argentine, Provini went to the final round in far-off Japan with high hopes of taking the 250 cc World title back to Italy. However, it was not to be, and after a series of problems, Provini had to accept 2nd place in the championships series, when he finished 4th in a race won by Honda team leader Redman.

Provini then left to join Benelli, and the youngster Giacomo Agostini was signed up for 1964.

Although he was unable to repeat Provini's success in the World series, the newcomer had the satisfaction of beating the former Morini star to take the Italian title. Although 'Ago' himself left to join MV in 1965, the Morini single was still competitive enough to win the 250 cc Senior Italian Championship in 1967, ridden by Angelo Bergamonti. It was then retired.

World Championships: None

In the years 1947, 1948 and 1949 the Morini factory offered this 125 Competitizione 'over-the-counter' racer. Like the works model, it was clearly based around the extremely successful pre-Second World War single-cylinder two-stroke German DKW design. Like the latter, the Morini featured piston port induction and full unit construction of the engine/gearbox unit, with three-speeds and crankshaft magneto ignition. The bike proved not only fast but reliable and was responsible for setting many budding Italian racers on their way to stardom, including Umberto Masetti.

Interesting view of Nello Pagani's 2nd place 125 Morini at the 1948 Dutch TT. This view shows to advantage its main features: piston port, three-speeds, unit construction engine with iron cylinder barrel; pressed steel 'blade' front forks; plunger rear suspension; and large capacity tank to enable races to be completed without refuelling.

Note the spark plug spanner inserted in the top of the rider's boot. This was usual among two-stroke racers of the day because of the fear of a fouled plug.

Morini

Dutch TT, 1 July 1948. Morini works rider Raffaele Alberti attends to his machine during the practice period. Alberti finished the 125 cc race in 4th spot. In front of him were the Dutch Eysink pair of Renooy (the winner) and Heineman (3rd). Another Morini rider, Nello Pagani, was 2nd. Earlier that year Alberti had won worldwide fame when together with a team of two other riders, he had helped establish 27 new world records with a 65 Guzzi two-stroke.

In 1949 Alfonso Morini designed and built a wholly new 123.1 cc (52 x 58 mm) single-cylinder machine, with chain-driven single overhead camshaft. It not only proved fast, but also won the 125 cc Italian Championships that year. In the classic events, however, things were different. The nearest Morini came to winning was in the Italian GP at Monza, where Umberto Masetti (pictured) came home 2nd. In 1950 Masetti joined Gilera and became Italy's first 500 cc World Champion.

Italian *Classic* Gallery

The leading Morini rider in the 1951 Italian GP at Monza was Luigi Zinzani, who split the dominant Mondial team to finish an impressive 3rd. His team mates Zanzi and Mendogni were placed 7th and 10th respectively: a lap adrift in the 16-lap 100.74 km (62.6 mile) race.

It is interesting to see Zinzani's rearward-placed feet: when changing gear or braking he had to adopt a more conventional posture.

Bottom left: Close-up view of the 1951-52 Morini 125 single overhead camshaft racing engine. By then it was providing 16 bhp at 9500 rpm (the original 1949 version gave 12 bhp) and it was good for a genuine 160 km/h (100 mph). Interesting features visible are the large oil tank and its cooler (just forward of the tank), oil pump, magneto (at the rear of the cylinder), and exposed hairpin valve springs. It could not be called a beautiful engine, but it was certainly efficient. Its best season was 1952, when Mendogni finished 3rd in the World Series.

Below: This experimental double overhead camshaft version of the 125 Morini racing engine appeared in 1952, but its development was halted as a result of the appearance of the new double-knocker MV Agusta and German NSU Rennfox.

At the end of the season the Morini factory retired from racing.

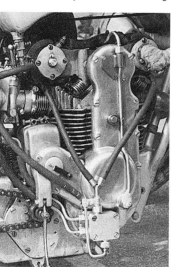

Morini

In the early 1950s Morini developed the 175 overhead valve Settebello sports roadster; then in 1955 came the more specialized Rebello. This had a 172.4 cc (60 x 61 mm) chain-driven single overhead valve engine. The Rebello was an immediate success, winning the 1955 Milan-Taranto and Giro d'Italia (Tour of Italy) long-distance road races – and the following year again took the Giro.

Following its success, the factory decided to build a 246.6 cc (69 x 66 mm) version and also fit a double overhead camshaft. The result was the 250 Rebello, which appeared in the autumn of 1957. The prototype of the new machine is seen on a factory bench that year. This first double overhead camshaft 250 Morini generated 29 bhp at 10,000 rpm.

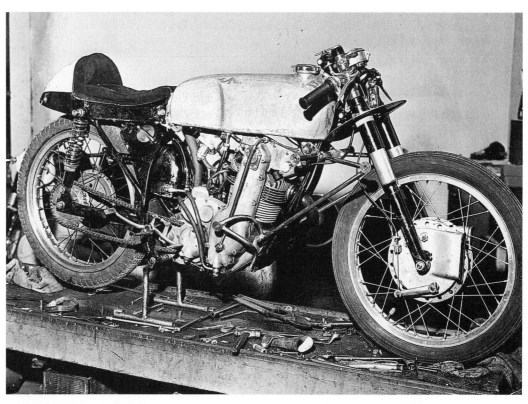

One of the very first outings for the new 250 double-knocker Morini single was at the international Coppa d'Oro Shell (Shell Gold Cup) meeting at Imola on Easter Monday, 7 April 1958. Ridden by Emilio Mendogni, the bike proved competitive, swapping places throughout the 28-lap 140.45 km (87.27 mile) race with the works MV Agusta pairing of Carlo Ubbiali and Tarquinio Provini.

Italian *Classic* Gallery

A vast crowd at Monza watch Emilio Mendogni score a sensational victory in the 250 cc class in the 1958 Italian Grand Prix. Like the Ducatis in the earlier 125 cc race, the Morini team showed the MV Agustas their speed right from the start. The first time around Mendogni and Zubani lay 1st and 3rd, with Masetti on another of the Bologna singles in 5th place. The MV pair of Provini (2nd) and Ubbiali (4th) made the filling in a double-decker sandwich; Masetti, however, soon had to retire with engine trouble. The other two Morini riders went on to finish a historic 1st and 2nd. Mendogni's average speed for the race was 168.21 km/h (104.52 mph); Zubani set the fastest lap at 171.07 km/h (106.30 mph).

Morini double overhead camshaft 250 cc engine as used by team riders in the 1958 Italian GP. Unlike the enlarged Rebello, it had the drive to its overhead camshafts by a train of gears running up the offside of the cylinder. Power was up to 32 bhp at 10,500 rpm. This was to be the basis for the successful engine campaigned in the 1960s, first by Provini, and later by Agostini.

Above: The 1957 500 cc World Champion, Libero Liberati, track-testing the Morini 250 at Monza in April 1959. In a team that included Mendogni and Britain's Derek Minter, Liberati's weight was a disadvantage on a lightweight bike such as the Morini: his best placing in a classic that year was a 4th at Hockenheim in West Germany.

A 1959 photograph of the 175 cc Morini Formula 3, single overhead camshaft racing engine. Note the deeply finned sump and generally smooth external lines of the unit construction design; also the selection of cams on the bench.

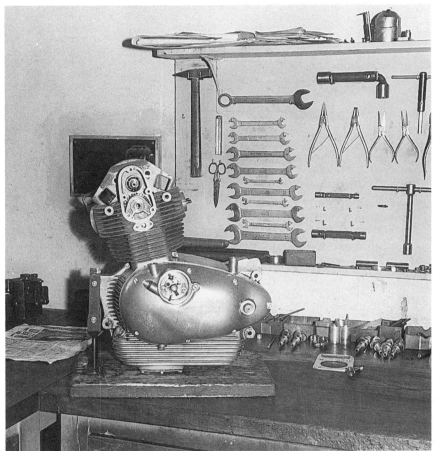

Future MV Agusta star Angelo Bergamonti with a 175 Morini production racer at Modena early in his career. Note also one of the fleet overhead valve Motobi flat singles in the picture.

Fresh from a magnificent victory in the 250 cc race on his double overhead camshaft Morini single at Imola on 16 April 1961, when he beat Ernst Degner (MZ), Silvio Grassetti (Benelli), Bruno Spaggiari (Benelli), Hans Fischer (MZ) and Tom Phillis (Honda), Tarquinio Provini rode in the Spanish GP at Barcelona a week later. Around the twisty Spanish circuit he held 2nd position, behind the flying Gary Hocking on a factory MV twin and ahead of the entire Honda, Benelli and MZ works teams. However, after trying a shade too hard, he came off and his race was over.

Hero of the 1962 Dutch TT at Assen was Morini's Tarquinio Provini, who voluntarily grounded his machine to avoid the Honda works rider Tommy Robb who, on his first outing on one of the Japanese fours, crashed early in the race. Although that cost him over half a minute, the Italian star failed to catch 2nd place man Bob McIntyre by a mere 0.4 sec, and set the fastest lap at 137.99 km/h (85.74 mph) in the process. The race was won by Honda team captain Jim Redman, who was 2.2 seconds in front of McIntyre. This race was to give a foretaste of what was to come the following year, when Provini challenged Redman for the 250 cc World title.

Above: The son of a garage proprietor, Tarquinio Provini was born on the 29 May 1933, in the village of Rovoleto di Cadeo in the province of Piacenza. As his early years were spent amid the engines and machinery of his father's workshop, it is hardly surprising that at just 10 years old, he was already riding a motorcycle. Too impatient to wait until he was old enough to hold a FIM racing licence, he appeared on the race circuit under his uncle's name: under this name he won the Italian Provincial Championships in both 1949 and 1950!

Top right: A line-up of machines in the Morini race shop during 1962. Besides the 250 Grand Prix bike in the foreground, there are machines for both Italian Junior events and sports category racing. In the centre of the picture is an ISDT-type machine with high handlebars and map case.

Right: Comm. Alfonso Morini (*left*), Angelo Bergamonti (in leathers) and Ing. Lambertini with the 250 Morini single at an Italian Championship meeting in 1967. That year the machine proved it was still in the top flight by winning the title, and in the process beating the Benelli four and Spanish Montesa twin.
After chalking up a massive number of victories over nine years the Morini company decided to retire from racing at the end of the season – much to their rivals' relief. Alfonso Morini died in 1969, leaving the Bologna factory in the hands of his daughter Gabrielli.

Italian *Classic* Gallery

Previously unpublished photographs of the superb 248.3 cc (72 x 61 mm) double overhead camshaft Morini single used by Provini in 1962 and 1963, and later in 1964 by the up-and-coming youngster Giacomo Agostini. These provide a rare glimpse of the technical masterpiece that lay behind the streamlining. It was designed by the former rider and gifted engineer Dante Lambertini. He had much useful assistance from Biavetti (formerly with the FB Mondial race team and a specialist in cylinder head gas flow). This definitive version of the Bologna single was good for 225 km/h (140 mph) – truly amazing for such an engine configuration.

Morini

The 250 cc West German GP at Solitude on Sunday 22 July 1964 was the setting for Giacomo Agostini's first venture abroad on his works Morini single. It proved to be quite a day: not only did he finish in 4th place behind Read (Yamaha), Redman (Honda) and Duff (Yamaha), but he was ahead of his forerunner at Morini, Tarquinio Provini on the Benelli four.

'Ago' averaged 154.19 km/h (95.81 mph), compared to race winner Redman's 156.11 km/h (97 mph), for the 11-lap 125.59 km/h (78.04 mile) race. The Solitude meeting was to be the only one abroad for Morini that year. Instead the team concentrated its efforts on the Italian Championships – and to good effect, as Agostini beat Provini to scoop the title.

This interesting racer was developed from the standard production 350 Sport roadster in 1975 by the British-based Devimead concern, headed by Les Mason. The capacity was increased from the original 344 cc to 460 cc, so that it could compete in 500 cc events. Although looking the part, the machine was dogged by mechanical problems centring around the big end and connecting rod assemblies. Mason even went to the trouble of employing a special pressed-up crankshaft, with one-piece connecting rods and roller bearing big end of Alpha design. However, even these failed to cure the problems.

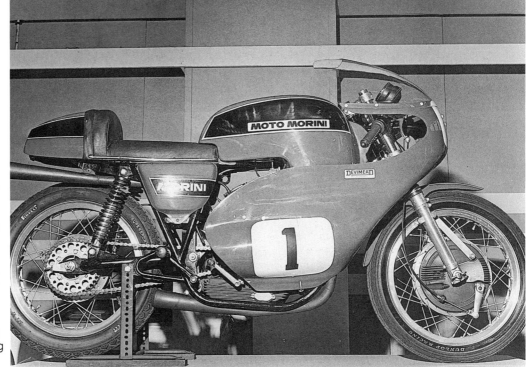

Moto Guzzi

The Guzzi contribution to the glamour and excitement of motorcycle racing has been a magnificent one in terms of both success and technical brilliance. From the firm's entry into racing in the early 1920s until its withdrawal in 1957, it favoured a horizontal single-cylinder engine layout, and with this basic design Guzzi machines and riders won ten TTs and eight World Championships.

Although Moto Guzzi achieved numerous Continental victories in its early days it was not until 1935, when Stanley Woods won both the Lightweight and Senior TTs, that Guzzi's efforts were crowned with truly International success. Other notable pre-war victories came in the 1937 Lightweight TT, and the epic defeat of the mighty

DKWs in the 1939 250 cc German Grand Prix.

Remaining faithful to the horizontal single-cylinder, Guzzi dominated the postwar 250 cc class from 1947 until 1953. Then the company enlarged the engine capacity, entered the 350 cc class and astounded the racing world by winning

Moto Guzzi's 250 Albatros. First produced in 1938, it was built until 1949 (the 1948 model is illustrated). This horizontal overhead camshaft single came into its own during the immediate postwar period, when its main rivals were effectively eliminated by the ban on superchargers – and the low-grade petrol available at the time. In Italy the only challengers to Guzzi supremacy were the Benelli and Parilla double overhead camshaft singles; but Guzzi usually came out on top.

The Albatros was used by both factory and private riders. Its capacity was 246.8 cc, with square 68 x 68 mm bore and stroke dimensions. Power output was 20 bhp at 7000 rpm, which gave the bike a maximum speed of around 177 km/h (110 mph).

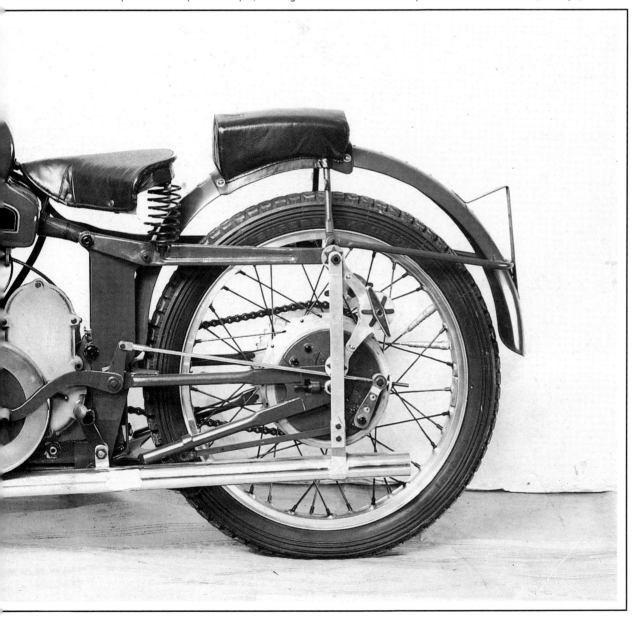

Italian Classic Gallery

the World Championship in the first year of participation.

Guzzi will always be remembered for its amazing versatility in design; for in addition to the famous singles it produced machines with V-twin, across-the-frame three-cylinder, inline four-cylinder and V-8 engines! Not content with that, the Mandello concern built a special wind tunnel to test and develop streamlining for its bikes, which contributed enormously to their racing and record-breaking successes.

The roll of famous riders that have achieved great victories on Guzzis is an impressive one: men such as Ghersi, Woods, Tenni, Sandri, Foster, Cann, Barrington, Ruffo, Lorenzetti, Anderson, Dale, Kavanagh, Lomas and Campbell, to name but a few.

When the factory retired from racing at the end of 1957, enthusiasts around the world realized that an era had come to an end.

World Championships: 250 cc 1949, 1951 and 1952; 350 cc 1953, 1954, 1955, 1956 and 1957

Omobono Tenni was without doubt the leading Italian rider of lightweight machinery in the years immediately prior to the outbreak of the Second World War. He was also the man who provided the first all-Italian TT victory, when he won the 250 cc racer over the tortuous 60.75 km (37.75 mile) Isle of Man Mountain circuit in 1937.

He is shown here with one of the 120° V-twin 500s at Gerona in the summer of 1945, in one of the very first meetings to be staged after the end of hostilities. Standing right is Count Giovanni Lurani, the great motor sporting enthusiast.

Moto Guzzi

Above: The popular Scot Fergus Anderson winning the 250 cc race at Ferrara, Italy, in May 1949. He began his racing career before the Second World War and soon resumed his track activities after its end.

He was a tower of strength in the Moto Guzzi line-up and contributed 12 out of 46 Grand Prix victories won by the Mandello del Lario factory.

Top right: Anderson after his 1949 victory at Ferrara. He is shown here riding through part of the town, flanked by members of the local police on 500 cc Gilera Saturnos. The photograph vividly recalls the atmosphere of road racing in Italy during the immediate postwar period.

Fergus Anderson pushes one of the wide-angle 500 Moto Guzzi V-twins into action at the Circuit de Nice, c. 1948. During this period the Scot rode both 250 and 500 Guzzis with great dash and determination throughout the length and breadth of Europe.

Italian *Classic* Gallery

The English rider Maurice Cann won the 250 cc Ulster Grand Prix on three consecutive occasions, 1948, 1949 and 1950, and went on to make it a fourth victory in 1952. All his wins were on Moto Guzzis. Cann is shown here at Clady Corner on his way to victory over the talented Bruno Ruffo on another Guzzi in the 1949 event, held on 20 August 1949. The postwar Clady circuit measured 16.5 miles. From the start there was a 3-mile stretch with a couple of fast curves leading to a pair of sharp rights at Nutts Corner; then a fast section of 2.5 miles to Tully Corner; more swerves, some fast and others slowish, to the very slow right-hand corner at Muckamore, almost 9 miles from the start. Then came the famous 7-mile Clady Straight, which was notorious for its bumps; finally, there was the slow Clady Corner and the fast run up to the finish of the lap.

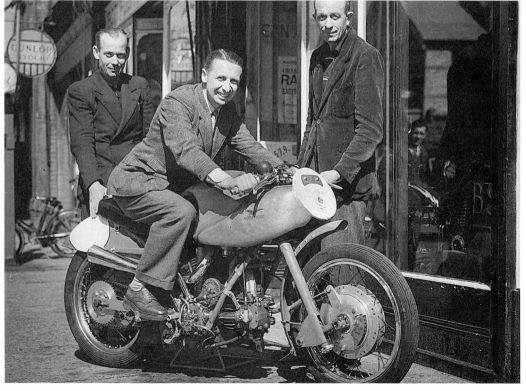

Bob Foster outside his Poole, Dorset showrooms before leaving for the Isle of Man in June 1950. The machine is a factory 500 cc Guzzi V-twin which he was scheduled to ride in the Senior TT. After holding 6th place, and averaging 140.22 km/h (87.13 mph) after 5 laps, the Moto Guzzi developed carburation problems, which progressively restricted its performance until he was forced to retire. For several years in the late 1940s and early 1950s Foster was the official Moto Guzzi agent for the British Isles. He also rode for Velocette, and it was with one of the latter machines that he became 350 cc World Champion in 1950.

Above: Born on 9 December 1920, Bruno Ruffo became the first 250 cc World Champion when he won the title in 1949. He is pictured here after winning the Swiss GP at Berne that year on a Moto Guzzi, covering 130 km (81 miles) distance in 1 hr 7.2 sec at an average speed of 130.71 km/h (81.22 mph).

He went on to win the 125 cc title on a Mondial in 1950 and the 250 cc (again on a Guzzi) the following year. A serious accident at Senigallia put paid to his 1952 season and another fall during the TT in 1953 brought his racing days to an end.

Top right: The 1951 version of Moto Guzzi's long-running 120°, 494.8 cc (68 x 68 mm) V-twin. Its history can be traced back to 1933. In 1935 came Stanley Woods' historic Senior TT victory on the machine and there were some equally famous victories both in Italy and abroad by Omobono Tenni.

After the Second World War the machine was revived, and modified each year until 1951 – its last year of competition. By then it was producing 48 bhp at 8000 rpm and gave a maximum speed of 210 km/h (130 mph). As well as Fergus Anderson's Swiss GP win, Bertacchini and Lorenzetti also had victories with it in its final year.

Exploded view of the various major components that went to make up the 1951 500 Moto Guzzi V-twin. Note in particular the two pairs of crankshaft flywheels, the bevel shaft drives for the overhead camshafts, hairpin valve springs and vertically split crankcases.

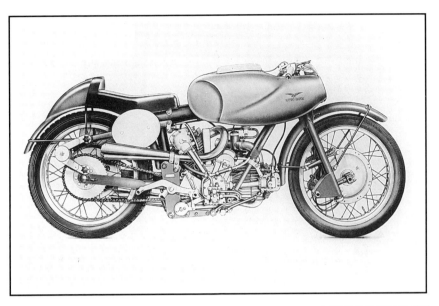

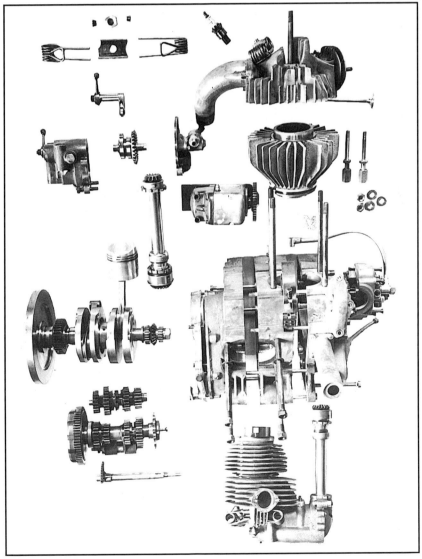

149

Italian *Classic* Gallery

The 1951 Moto Guzzi works team, *left to right:* Bruno Ruffo, Fergus Anderson, Enrico Lorenzetti and Gianni Leoni.
Ruffo became 250 cc World Champion that year and Lorenzetti took the title in 1952. Anderson's turn came in 1953 and 1954, when he won a pair of 350 cc championships.
Sadly, Leoni and another Moto Guzzi rider, Sante Geminiani were killed during unofficial practice for the Ulster GP in August 1951.

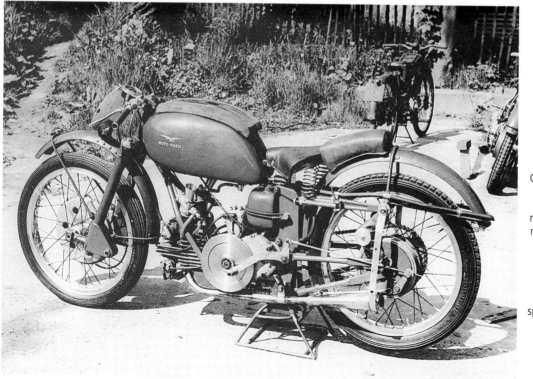

Experimental four-valve 260 cc Moto Guzzi with twin Dell'Orto carburettors used by Fergus Anderson in practice for the 1951 Junior TT. He did not ride it in the race, however, as he did not feel it was capable of completing the seven laps of the 60.75 km (37.75 mile) Isle of Man Mountain circuit. As events were to prove, however, the real significance of this machine's appearance is that it spurred the factory to go on to build, first a 317 cc, then a 345 cc, and finally a 349 cc version with which Guzzi was to gain five successive 350 cc World Championships (1953-7).

Moto Guzzi

Ultimate version of the Moto Guzzi Gambalunghino ('Little Long-leg'), with works rider Fergus Anderson doing a spot of testing at the Ospidaletti circuit, San Remo, in February 1952.

Below right: The experimental 1952 Bialbero (double camshaft) 250 Moto Guzzi engine assembly. Note the widely splayed angle for mounting the two carburettors, outside flywheel and enclosed valve gear.

Below: Enrico Lorenzetti with the spoils of victory after winning the 250 cc Italian Grand Prix at Monza, 9 September 1951. Lorenzetti's win came after the leader Bruno Ruffo had been slowed down by a bad oil leak; then the British rider Tommy Wood (also on a Guzzi) with only 200 yds before the finishing line, in front of the packed grandstands, calmly shut his throttle, sat up, and let Lorenzetti through to a win he hardly deserved. Obviously riding to factory team orders! All of the first six riders home were Moto Guzzi-mounted.

Italian *Classic* Gallery

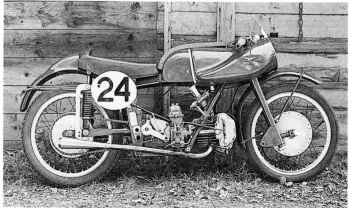

Top left: Commissioned in 1951, the Moto Guzzi wind tunnel at the Mandello del Lario works was completed in 1952. It was to play a vital role in providing the company with the technical data necessary to attain a world lead in the art of streamlining. Guzzi made full use of its facilities until retiring from the sport at the end of 1957. Thereafter it was hired out to other companies, and later still used in the development of production roadsters in the 1970s and '80s.

Top right: The prototype double-knocker 250 Moto Guzzi first tested in 1952. It was built to replace the Gambalunghino, but with the arrival of the German NSU Rennmax twin, it was soon retired. Even so, in 1953 Anderson won the Lightweight TT with it, and Lorenzetti managed victories at Monza and Barcelona. The machine shown had four valves and twin carburettors. The bikes that were raced, however, were far more conservative, with a single carburettor and two valves.

Fergus Anderson again at Ospidaletti, this time in early 1953 with one of the 'bird beak' streamlined 250s the Guzzi works raced that year – its first public appearance. The same streamlining was used on the 350 cc class machines in 1953.

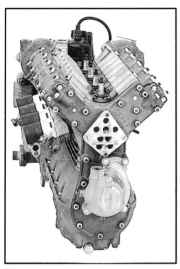

Above: The 500 cc in line four-cylinder engine which Moto Guzzi commissioned from the Rome engineer Ing. Carlo Gianini. If speed had been the only priority, it is likely that this power plant would have gained more success than it actually achieved. Enrico Lorenzetti proved this by winning the first big event in which a bike powered by this unit appeared: an international at Hockenheim, West Germany, in May 1953. He averaged 173 km/h (107.5 mph), and team mate Fergus Anderson on a second machine put in the fastest lap at 181.85 km/h (113 mph). On slower, twistier circuits, however, this bike was less effective.

Top right: Englishman Tommy Wood on his privately entered Moto Guzzi winning in France in April 1953. Wood rode 250 Guzzi s for several years, and also a MK VIII KTT Velocette. He was a leading member of the Continental Circus.

Right: The former Norton star Ken Kavanagh joined Moto Guzzi at the beginning of 1954. The Australian is shown here on 25 February 1954 with one of the new 499 cc (88 x 82 mm) double overhead camshaft horizontal singles. Raced until the end of 1957 (even though Guzzi also had the sensational V-8 for most of this period), the big single pumped out 42 bhp at 7000 rpm. The combination of light weight, superb handling, good reliability and excellent penetration ensured some leader board positions against the best multi-cylinder racers of the era, such as the Gilera and MV Agusta fours.

153

Italian *Classic* Gallery

Inset: The 1954 version of the famous 349.2 cc (80 x 69.5 mm) double-knocker single, which Moto Guzzi introduced that year. Designed by the legendary Ing. Giulio Cesare Carcano, it was the dominant force in its class and won the 350 cc world title each year until 1957, when with Gilera and Mondial, Moto Guzzi announced its retirement from the sport.

Below: Top privateer Arthur Wheeler. A motorcycle dealer from Epsom, Surrey, Wheeler rode a variety of 250 Guzzi singles for a decade from 1952 until he retired at the end of 1962. He is shown here at Silverstone in the mid-1950s.

The bike illustrated still has the standard Guzzi chassis; later Wheeler used special Reynolds frames and forks in his attempt to remain competitive against the newest machinery.

Cecil Sandford (2) with the ex-works 250 Guzzi double overhead camshaft he rode in 1954 and 1955. It was built in 1953 and is shown here about to pip Arthur Wheeler on a single camshaft model for 2nd place at the important Silverstone Saturday meeting held on 23 April 1955. The race was won by John Surtees with a German NSU Sportmax.

Italian *Classic* Gallery

At Montlhéry, near Paris, on 23 March 1955, a 348 cc Moto Guzzi took 22 world records. The riders were Anderson, Dale, Kavanagh and Agostini. The machine used was essentially one of the 1953 single overhead camshaft racers with a special dolphin fairing. The later, more comprehensive streamlining was not employed because during long-distance record attempts, speedy access to the wheels for tyre changing was necessary.

Anderson got things under way at 7.30 am in heavy rain and rode for the first hour, to be followed by Dale, Kavanagh and Agostini, each for hour-long periods. After almost 10 hours, with Agostini in the saddle, the oil tank ran dry. The result was severe damage to the engine. A distance of 1697.05 km (1054.5 miles) had been covered, sufficient to claim the 11- and 12-hour records. Also gained were the 8- and 9-hour records. The 1000 mile distance was covered at an average of 173.68 km/h (107.92 mph). All these figures also applied to the 500 cc, 750 cc and 1000 cc classes. The team also broke the existing 12-hour record for the 350 and 500 cc categories with an average of 141.43 km/h (87.88 mph) – even though they were 2 hours short! Our photograph shows Moto Guzzi's chief designer Ing. Carcano and riders Dale and Kavanagh.

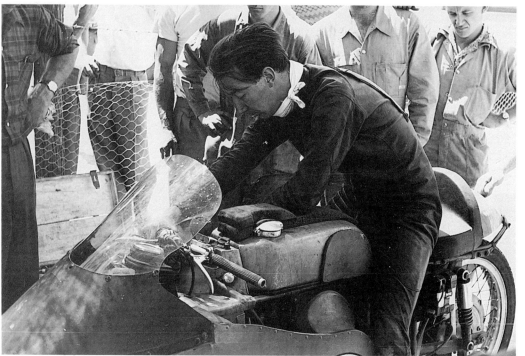

During the close season, 1955-6 Moto Guzzi permitted its works riders Bill Lomas and Dickie Dale to spend the winter months racing in Australia (as Anderson had done years before). The machines taken were both singles, a 350 and 500. Both were modified to run on straight methanol and the compression ratios raised accordingly. This enabled the riders to compete more effectively with the numbers of local riders using similar fuel.

Lomas is shown here warming up one of the bikes before a successful foray on to the circuit.

Moto Guzzi

Bill Lomas gets a flyer at the start of the Junior race in the Australian TT, January 1956. Also in the picture are a collection of AJS, Norton and BSA Velocette singles.

The peak of design achievement in the 1950s, that golden era of postwar motorcycle road racing, was represented by the Moto Guzzi V-8, by the brilliant Ing. Carcano.

The 498.7 cc (44 x 41 mm) power unit with gear-driven double overhead camshaft and water-cooling, was the most advanced motorcycle engine of its time.

With a wide spread of power (between 7000 and 12,000 rpm) it only needed a four-speed gearbox. Its speed was phenomenal – so long as it kept going. Raced in 1956 and 1957, it was not fully developed when the factory pulled out of racing at the end of 1957.

Italian *Classic* Gallery

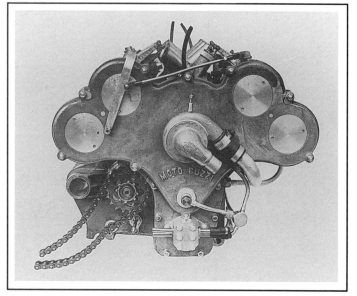

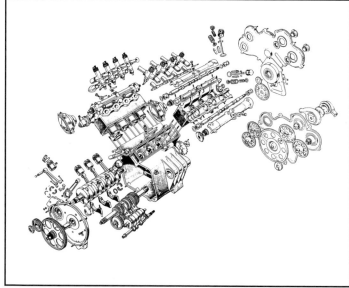

Top left: Side view of the 75 bhp V-8. Before retiring it was timed at 286 km/h (178 mph) on the straight during the 1957 500 cc Belgian Grand Prix.

Above: Exploded view of the Moto Guzzi 90° V-8 power unit. For such a potentially complex design the layout was amazingly uncluttered; a fitting tribute to Ing. Carcano's engineering talents.

The 1957 350 cc World Champion Keith Campbell rode this 500 Moto Guzzi single in the 1957 Senior TT. After finishing 2nd to Bob McIntyre (Gilera) in the Junior race, Campbell rode brilliantly to finish a very creditable 5th on the larger capacity single, averaging 150.10 km/h (93.27 mph) for the extended 8-lap event – specially lengthened to commemorate the Isle of Man's Jubilee TT races (1907-57).
Another Guzzi finished 4th. This was the V-8 model ridden by Dickie Dale. It finished on only seven cylinders.

Moto Guzzi

A massive two-day, high-speed operation, organized by Moto Guzzi on the Monza banked track on 30 and 31 October 1969, resulted in a further 15 world records in the solo and sidecar classes being taken by the Mandello del Lario factory, which was making a return to a race circuit after an absence of 12 years.

To enable the firm to capture records in both the 750 and 1000 cc classes, two engine sizes were prepared: 739.3 cc (82 x 70 mm) and 757.5 cc (83 x 70 mm).

The most significant result came on 31 October, when Alberto Pagani (shown) on the larger-engined machine set new standards for the 1000 cc class, with 218.40 km/h (135.71 mph) for the 100 km distance; and 1 hour at 233.44 km/h (138.84 mph). The latter figure might well have been even higher if Pagani, delayed at the start by last-minute adjustments to the carburation, had not met fog and darkness in the last quarter of an hour.

At the Imola 200 Miles on 23 April 1972, three works 750 Moto Guzzis appeared. Prepared in just six weeks by a team led by Ing. Lino Tonti, they finished 8th, 10th and 11th, ridden by Vittorio Brambrilla, Jack Findlay and Guido Mandracci.

The engines, based on the production V-7 Sport model, were tuned to give around 80 bhp and the riders revved them to 8400 rpm in the gears and 8000 rpm in top.

Guzzi employed a new type of Dell'Orto and experimented with both 38 and 40 mm carburettors. Also used were double-disc front brakes and a disc rear brake, with Lockheed calipers.

Our photograph shows the Australian Findlay in action.

MV Agusta

The Agusta name has long been associated with the aviation industry and is today not only Italy's main helicopter manufacturer, but also one of the most important in the world.

For 30 years, from 1945 to 1975, it was also a big name in the world of racing motorcycles.

MV (Meccanica Verghera) Agusta's first racing efforts were centred around a relatively simple two-stroke, piston port single, which was campaigned with mixed success until the end of 1949.

MV Agusta's first four-stroke models, a 125 single and a 500 four, appeared in 1950, after the Gilera designer Remor joined the firm.

The next big step was the signing of the 1949 500 cc World Champion, the Englishman Les Graham, who joined the Gallarate concern for the 1951 season. It is Graham who is widely acknowledged as the man who did the most to develop the legendary 'fire engine' four-cylinder model into an effective racing machine during those early days.

After finishing 2nd in the TT, and with victories in the Spanish and Italian Grands Prix in 1952, it then seemed as though the factory was all set for the Championship in 1953, but MV's plans were shattered by Graham's tragic death in the Senior TT.

Les Graham had moved to Italy with his family to live near the MV plant, and Count Domenico Agusta showed his respect for the

In the first year of the new World Championship series in 1949, MV Agusta fielded a team of riders on 123.5 cc (53 x 56 mm) single-cylinder, piston port two-strokes, one of which is seen in the paddock at the Italian GP at Monza that year. The team comprised Ubbiali, Bertoni and Matucchi. The best placing was a 3rd by Ubbiali in Holland. After finishing in 3rd place in the 1949 and 1950 Championships, Ubbiali left to join rivals FB Mondial with whom he won his first title in 1951. Back with MV from 1953 onwards, he went on to gain another eight World Championships, making nine in all.

English rider by withdrawing the larger capacity MVs from most of the other races for the remainder of the 1953 season.

For 1954 the Count signed the former Norton star, Rhodesian Ray Amm, in an attempt to gain Championship honours, but in this very first race for his new employer he, too, was killed. Then came a succession of riders until at last, in 1956, the Gallarate concern had the right kind of luck when John Surtees was signed up. Surtees responded brilliantly by winning the 500 cc World title at his first attempt; and it was Surtees who, after Gilera and Guzzi withdrew in 1957, went on to dominate the 350 and 500 cc classes for the next three seasons.

In the two lightweight classes MV was no less successful, winning a host of championships between 1951 and 1960, thanks in no small part to the brilliance of the rider Carlo Ubbiali.

In later years MV withdrew from the smaller classes in the face of the rising Oriental tide; but men such as Hocking, Hailwood, Agostini, and finally Read, ensured that in the 350 and 500 cc categories the Gallarate factory went on to become the most successful marque in the history of the World Championship series, winning a total of 37 titles.

World Championships: 37 in all categories

MV Agusta built this heavily streamlined shell to house one of its works double-knocker 125 engines for an attack on the class speed record. However, tragedy struck when its pilot, Carlo Maggi, was fatally injured in an accident while testing near Rome on 17 April 1951.

Italian *Classic* Gallery

December 1950, and the MV Agusta team for the following year assemble. *Left to right:* four mechanics, Count Domenico Agusta, Ing. Remor, Les Graham, Corrado Agusta, Mario Agusta, Giuseppina Agusta, Franco Bertacchini and Carlo Bandirola. The machine is one of the first four-cylinder MVs 500s to be constructed. Although of inferior quality, this photograph is included for its rarity value.

Englishman Les Graham joined the MV team at the end of 1950. His first season was dogged by mechanical failure, typified by his retirement in both his rides (125 and 500 cc) in the Italian GP that year. He is seen here at Monza with his smaller mount. Like the four-cylinder model, this was the work of Ing. Remor. Its 123.5 cc (53 x 56 mm) double overhead camshaft engine was housed in a duplex frame with swinging arm rear suspension and blade front forks. The disc-type rear wheel and handlebar fairing were soon discarded.

Above: First outing for MV Agusta 'new' boy Les Graham was the Spanish GP at Barcelona in early April 1951. He is seen here (in helmet) looking on as Ing. Remor and mechanic Arturo Magni make adjustments to the 500 cc four-cylinder machine.

In the race itself, after gobbling up places following a poor start, Graham got up to 3rd position on lap 7 of the 34-lap, 204 km (127 mile) event, only to drop out on the next circuit with gear selector trouble

Right: Graham's MV Agusta four at the 1951 Spanish Grand Prix at Montjuich Park, Barcelona. Some of the more important technical features of the design are clearly visible in the photograph, including the dual Dell'Orto carburettors with separate float chambers; Lucas racing magneto; sand cast crankcase assembly; exhaust system; and parallelogram (double) torsion bar rear suspension with friction absorbers.

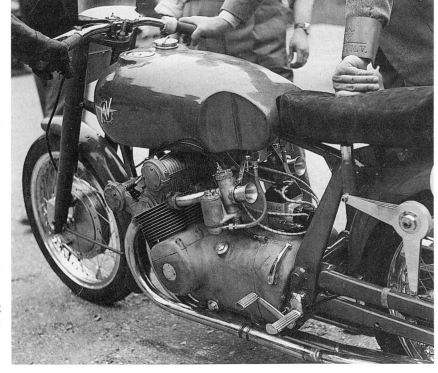

Above: Both team leader Graham and Bandirola (seen here sitting astride machine number 50) used these special fairings, which enclosed the steering head and front portion of the fuel tank of their machines at the Italian Grand Prix in the last of the classic races for 1951, at Monza. Bandirola was the only MV Agusta finisher, back in 9th place, a lap adrift of the race winner, Milani's Gilera.

Left: Technical details of the 1953 MV Agusta 125. With a capacity of 123.5 cc (53 x 53 mm), maximum power was around 17 bhp at 11,000 rpm, and the gearbox was a five-speeder. Of special interest is the massive cover running up the side of the engine. This housed the train of gears that drove the double overhead camshafts. Also clearly visible is the large-capacity oil tank for the dry sump lubrication system, with a mass of oil pipes running to the oil pump. This can be seen at the front of the crankcase. Behind is the magneto, in a position that afforded some protection from the elements.

MV Agusta

For the 1953 racing season MV Agusta decided to construct for sale to private owners a single overhead camshaft version of its 1952 World Championship-winning bike, which had been used so successfully by the English rider Cecil Sandford to win the first title for the Gallerate factory. The machine, the Sport Competizione, featured an engine with identical capacity and bore/stroke measurements 123.55 cc (53 x 56 mm) to the Works bike, as well as most of its other technical features – including the multi-plate clutch, geared primary drive, gear-driven oil pump and dry sump, 27 mm Dell'Orto carburettor, and a long, shallow tapered megaphone exhaust. Unfortunately for buyers of the 'over-the-counter' racer its power was considerably less (12 bhp at 10,000 rpm), and its four-speed box had one less ratio than that on the factory double-knocker.

After two years with Mondial, Carlo Ubbiali returned to MV Agusta for 1953. He is pictured here making his début at an Italian Championship meeting on 26 March 1953. Although he was destined to gain the Italian 125 cc Senior Championship that year, his double overhead camshaft MV Agusta single was not quick enough to challenge the German NSUs in the World title chase – even though he won the German GP at Schotten. He eventually finished the season in 3rd place in the World series.

Main picture: In the German GP at Solitude on 25 July 1954, there was a battle royal for 2nd place in the 125 cc race between Carlo Ubbiali MV (162) and Werner Haas NSU (167). The German eventually took the position, with the Italian 3rd. Time after time Haas and Ubbiali changed places; as the pair swept into the finishing straight at the conclusion of each lap they presented a stirring sight, riding abreast on their sleek, fully streamlined machines. The race was won by another NSU rider, Ruppert Hollaus, at 126.93 km/h (78.87 mph).

Inset: Persistent clutch slip slowed the new 350 MV Agusta four when it made its début in the 1953 Junior TT. Rider Les Graham is seen here at high speed on the Mountain road. After two comparatively slow laps he retired on reaching his pit. During the Senior Isle of Man race, Graham lost control of his larger MV four coming down Bray Hill. In the ensuing crash he was killed instantly. At the time he was lying 2nd behind leader Geoff Duke on a Gilera, but he too crashed out and the race was won by the Norton star, Ray Amm.

Italian *Classic* Gallery

This was one of several fairings tested by MV Agusta during the mid-1950s. Works rider Carlo Bandirola is seen here during the 500 cc race of the Italian Championships, held at Senigallia, August 1954. Using the same form of streamlining, Bandirola had finished 3rd in the Dutch TT in June that year.

The four-cylinder 350 MV after the accident that claimed the life of the former Norton star, Ray Amm. The crash occurred during the 350 cc race at Imola on Easter Monday, 11 April 1955. It was Amm's first big race since joining the MV team earlier that year. The 27-year-old Ray Amm had come to Britain, from what was then Southern Rhodesia, in 1951 for the Isle of Man TT races, and had subsequently become one of the world's top riders. He had an especially aggressive style and was probably one of the hardest riders ever to appear on a race circuit. The death of Ray Amm was almost as big a blow to MV as that of Les Graham two years earlier. It was not until the signing of John Surtees that the team was to manage a recovery.

The first British appearance of the new 1956 model MV Agusta 500 four, with its new rider John Surtees, was at the Crystal Palace circuit in South East London on Easter Monday, 2 April.

The engine was similar to the earlier version, but had been modified to provide increased power: almost 70 bhp at 10,500 rpm, giving it a top speed of around 250 km/h (155 mph). Also improved was the frame, which not only offered superior handling, but was lower and lighter too. Forks were now of the leading axle telescopic variety.

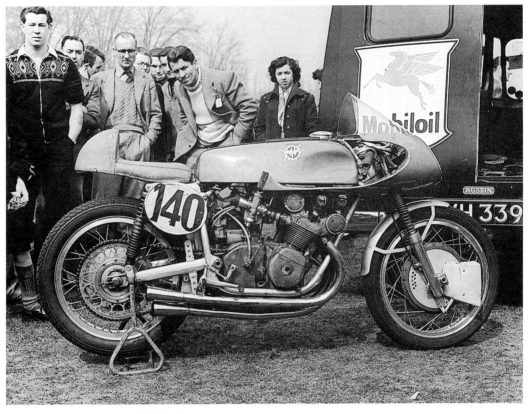

Surtees got off to a cracking start in the 1956 500 cc World Championship series by winning the Senior TT. He is shown here on his way to victory over the famous 60.75 km (37.75 mile) Isle of Man Mountain circuit. It was also the first time the big MV Agusta showed that it had not only speed, but staying power too. Surtees' time for the seven-lap, 425.08 km (264.13 mile) race was 2 hr 44 min 5.8 sec, an average speed of 157.02 km/h (97.57 mph). He also set the fastest lap at 157.38 km/h (97.79 mph). Surtees, who was born on 11 February 1934, won the first three rounds (the Isle of Man, the Dutch TT and Belgian GP) before taking a tumble in the 350 cc class of the German GP at Solitude, thus putting himself out of contention for the rest of the season. Even so, he had collected enough points to carry off the Championship. This was not only Surtees' first World title, but MV's first in the all-important 500 cc category.

Left: MV Agusta's new signing John Surtees with the MV Agusta 500 four, at Crystal Palace, 2 April 1956.

After an impressive period on single cylinder Manx Nortons, Surtees came to the attention of Count Domenico Agusta through his British talent scout Bill Webster. Throughout the 1950s Webster had close ties with the Agusta factory. As well as racing 125 and 250 semi-works MVs, he also acted as the unofficial importer for the 'over-the-counter' racers before the appointment of MV Concessionairese headed by Ron Harris in late 1955. Later Webster became Britain's first Aermacchi importer.

Top right: A race that was to see John Surtees (76) suffer a nasty crash, which left him with a broken left arm: the 1956 350 cc German GP. Surtees is shown here leading the eventual race winner, Bill Lomas (88), on a Moto Guzzi flat single.

The young Londoner had in fact also fallen in the final practice session for the class the day before the race and the frame on his MV four had been twisted. The engine had hurriedly been built into a spare chassis.

Right: Monza, August 1957. MV Agusta team manager Nello Pagani about to test the new 500 six-cylinder model. However, the withdrawal of the Gilera and Moto Guzzi teams at the end of that year meant that it was never needed. This rare photograph is one of only a few in existence and probably the only one showing the original full 'dustbin' streamlining, which was banned by the FIM shortly afterwards.

Another view of the 'King of the lightweights', Carlo Ubbiali. He is shown here at Cronk y Caroo on the Isle of Man Clyse circuit, during the 125 cc TT in 1958. His victory came only after a furious MV – Ducati battle for supremacy. This was the year when Ducati made an all-out bid for championship honours.

At the start of the race, Ubbiali and Provini on MV Agustas lined up against the Desmo Ducatis of Ferri, Taveri, Chadwick and Miller. Early in the race Taveri led, hounded by Ubbiali, with Provini a close 3rd. Behind them came Miller, Chadwick and Fugner (MZ). The *Motor Cycle* in its race report commented, 'A newspaper would have covered the lot'. The pace was so hot that both Taveri and Provini were eventually to retire, leaving Ubbiali to win from Ferri, Chadwick and Miller.

John Hartle with his 350 MV Agusta four at the assembly area behind the grandstands at Douglas, Isle of Man. 1958 was to be a fruitless year for Hartle, for in both races he was doomed to be a non-finisher. In the Junior TT a piston disintegrated at the Bungalow on the first lap; in the Senior his machine caught fire and was burned out!

Above: The 250 cc Lightweight TT, 3 June 1959. Carlo Ubbiali leads Tarquinio Provini. Both are mounted on single-cylinder models (even though by then an MV twin existed). Provini duplicated the result of the 1958 race by heading home team mate Ubbiali. His average speed was a record at 125.16 km/h (77.77 mph), yet he won by no more than 0.4 sec. Lap records, too, were shattered. But what really made the day was the ferocious ride by Mike Hailwood, who hurled his ex-works Mondial past both the MV stars and with two laps to go seemed all set to win. The effort failed when his engine refused to take further punishment; but it was an electrifying spectacle while it lasted.

Top right: Surtees studies one of the MV Agusta fours he rode to a double victory in the 350 and 500 cc Ulster GPs held over the 11.94 km (7.42 mile) Dundrod circuit on the hilltops above Belfast. Unchallenged, he averaged 146.97 km/h (91.32 mph) in the smaller category event and 153.34 km/h (95.28 mph) in the Blue Riband 500 cc race.

Right: In the Italian Grand Prix at Monza on 6 September 1959, John Surtees scored yet another 350/500 cc double for MV Agusta. Second place in both races was taken by Remo Venturi (to Surtees' right in the photograph). The English rider raised the lap record to 191.83 km/h (119.2 mph).

Italian *Classic* Gallery

Inset right: Carlo Ubbiali with his wife on the podium after winning the 250 cc race in the 1959 Italian GP. The machine he used for this victory was the new 247 cc (53 x 56 mm) double overhead camshaft twin. Compared with the 250 single, the new model had an extra 3-4 bhp and revved to 12,500 rpm. Even though there was the odd victory for the East German MZ two-stroke, Ubbiali won both the 1959 and 1960 250 cc World titles on MV's 215 km/h (135 mph) twin. However, after Ubbiali had announced his retirement at the end of 1960, Gary Hocking was to gain only a single victory on the machine before the Honda onslaught ended its career.

Inset far right: For 1960 MV Agusta had three riders in the larger classes: Surtees, Venturi, and new boy Gary Hocking, from what was then called Southern Rhodesia. At first the Count would not let Hocking loose on the 500. For example, at the French GP, held over the sinuous 8 km (5 mile) Clermont-Ferrand circuit, Hocking only rode an overbored 250 twin, with a capacity of 282 cc, in the 350 cc event.

As our photograph shows, only Surtees (his machine is furthest from the camera) and Venturi took part in the 500 cc race. They finished 1st and 2nd, averaging 121.60 km/h (75.56 mph) and 118.01 km/h (73.33 mph) respectively. The MV pair lapped all the other competitors at least once in the 13-lap, 104.72 km (65.07 mile) race.

Main picture: Senior TT, Isle of Man, 6 June 1958. John Hartle watches as his MV Agusta four begins to blaze at Governor's Bridge. At 12.39 pm, just as he was about to complete his fourth lap, Hartle was forced to abandon his machine. It was totally destroyed in the fire, even though the marshal (*left*) tried his best with a fire extinguisher. A dejected Hartle stands well away (*far right*) unable to prevent the destruction of the machine. The fire was caused by a split fuel tank.

Italian *Classic* Gallery

John Surtees in typically smooth style on his way to victory in the 500 cc French Grand Prix at Clermont-Ferrand on 22 May 1960, the first round of the World Championship series. At the end of the season, with another 350/500 cc double, he retired from the sport and began a new career on four wheels. He became the first and only man to win the top laurels in both branches of motorized sport, for he took the World Formula One title in 1964 at the wheel of a Ferrari. In 1969 he founded his own racing team and achieved further success in 1973 as a manufacturer of Formula One cars.

The Belgian GP, 3 July 1960. John Surtees at La Source hairpin in the 500 cc event. He displayed his skill most vividly by not only dominating the race, but by boosting the lap record to 197.45 km/h (122.69 mph). In a field of 26, Surtees led from start to finish; in fact he was so far in front that he might almost have been competing in another race. His was a one-man, high-speed demonstration. Team mate Remo Venturi was 2nd throughout, conceding many seconds a lap, but untroubled by the rest of the field who were mainly mounted on single-cylinder Nortons.

MV Agusta

'Mike-the-Bike' Hailwood powers his works MV Agusta four around Coram Curve at the Snetterton circuit in Norfolk on Easter Sunday 1962, on his way to victory in the 500 cc race. It was his first-ever race in Britain on the Gallarate 'fire engine'. The news, which created headlines all over Britain, brought spectators in thousands to the Snetterton Combine's national meeting over the 4.36 km (2.71 mile) circuit.

They were not disappointed. Hailwood won both his races and was in supreme form. He set new lap records in both classes – with the 500 cc in 1 min 41.4 sec, a speed of 154.83 km/h (96.21 mph).

This new 125 cc two-stroke MV Agusta made a brief appearance in practice at Cesenatico, a road circuit on the Adriatic coast, in the international meeting held there on 5 May 1965. Ridden by future World Champion Walter Villa, the new MV was to strike gearbox trouble and so rule itself out of the racing. Villa rode one of the old double overhead camshaft four-stroke singles in the race to finish 5th behind Degner (Suzuki), brother Francesco Villa (Mondial), Mandolini (Mondial) and Visenzi (Mondial).

In fact the MV Agusta two-stroke, designed by West German engineer Peter Durr, followed the same lines as the Mondial of the period, with its horizontal cylinder and rotary valve induction. However, it proved unreliable and was soon scrapped.

Italian *Classic* Gallery

At the end of 1964 Count Agusta signed up the promising young Morini rider Giacomo Agostini. 'Ago' soon showed his ability by not only leading the 350 cc World Championship series for much of 1965, but also putting in a number of appearances in the 500 category. He is shown here finishing 2nd behind Mike Hailwood in the Dutch TT that year on the larger MV.

MV Agusta introduced its new three-cylinder racer in the 350 cc class for the 1965 season. One of the machines is shown here, minus its fairing, at the Italian GP at Monza on 8 September 1965. With four valves per cylinder, the double overhead camshaft triple displaced 349.2 cc (55 x 49 mm) and revved to over 12,000 rpm. Maximum power was around 58 bhp. A seven-speed gearbox was fitted. The cylindrical object between the camshaft boxes is an oil filter. Agostini won the race at an average speed of 181.90 km/h (113.03 mph) and team mate Hailwood on another three, set a new lap record of 189.39 km/h (117.68 mph).

Right: Agostini pilots the new 500 MV Agusta three-cylinder in the Czech GP in 1966. Although he finished the race in 2nd place behind Mike Hailwood, he went on to become 500 cc World Champion that year, the first of many as an MV Agusta rider.

The 491.2 cc (60.5 x 57 mm) engine followed the design of the smaller triple, with its gear-driven double overhead camshaft and four valves per cylinder. Maximum power was 80 bhp at 12,000 rpm.

Bottom right: Giacomo Agostini in winning form at Brands Hatch, October 1966. His riding style was not spectacular, but clean. Although he was no giant he naturally took to the big MV – a machine that called for considerable physical effort to handle successfully.

Below: Giacomo Agostini was born in Brescia, northern Italy on 16 June 1942, the eldest of four brothers, but he lived most of his childhood in Lovere, on the shore of Lake Iseo. It was in this setting that the young Giacomo got his first taste of motorcycling. There was a particular winding road behind his village, which probably accounts for the fact that his first speed event was in the Trento-Bondon hillclimb. That was in 1961 at the age of 19. During 1962 he took up road racing and one of his most impressive wins came in the Bologna-San Luca, where on his 175 Morini, he dominated the event and was offered a works ride. His successes for Morini led to the MV signing for 1965.

Top left: Agostini during the 1967 Senior TT. He is shown here at Brandish some 57 km (35.5 miles) out. On his larger 491.2 cc (60.5 x 57 mm) three-cylinder model he shattered the lap record from a standing start at 174.74 km/h (108.58 mph), only to have it beaten by Hailwood (Honda) a lap later at 175.05 km/h (108.77 mph). Agostini was to retire with only one lap to go while leading Hailwood by 2 seconds.

Above: Early 1967 and Agostini (MV) leads Renzo Pasolini's Benelli four in an Italian Senior Championship meeting at Cesenatico on the Adriatic coast. This was one of the most popular of the Italian street circuits during the 1960s.

Agostini again, this time receiving the victor's garlands after winning the 'Race of the Year' at Mallory Park in September 1967.

Another Agostini shot – this time he is winning the Redex Trophy race at Brands Hatch, 5 October 1969. That year had seen him complete another 350 and 500 cc double in the World Championship series. The only opponent capable of mounting a challenge had been the diminutive Bill Ivy, but sadly he was killed at the Sachsenring, East Germany, when his 350 Jawa V-four seized. Ago dominated the 500 cc class completely, with a total number of points three times greater than his closest rival.

Bottom right: The final Grand Prix of 1970 was held in Barcelona, Spain, on the weekend of 26 and 27 September. With both the 350 and 500 cc World titles already secured by team leader Giacomo Agostini, the former Aermacchi star Angelo Bergamonti was given the responsibility of upholding MV honour. He responded magnificently by winning both races. Bergamonti is seen here with the bigger three-cylinder model during his winning ride.

Below: Brands Hatch, on an October day in 1967. Giacomo Agostini awaits the start in sombre mood.

Top left: Start of the 1973 350 cc Finnish Grand Prix at Imatra. The works MVs are Agostini (1) and Phil Read (5). Both the race and the title were won by the Italian, his 13th. With victory also in the 500 cc race that followed Agostini had amassed a record-breaking 108 GP victories. Later a fall at Misano, during a private practice session, prevented him from taking part in the final round in Spain. In 1974 Agostini was to move to Yamaha, the marque that had caused him many problems in 1973. His former team mate Phil Read was now his principal adversary, on the machine with which he had achieved so much success – the MV Agusta.

Top right: His last ride before joining Yamaha: Agostini rides his four-cylinder MV Agusta to victory in the 500 cc Finnish Grand Prix, 29 July 1973.

Rider's eye view: the cockpit of a works MV Agusta, c. 1973. Note the large white face 4000-18,000 rpm Veglia tachometer, adjustable damping for front forks, massive steering damper control unit and quick-action fuel filler.

Nicknamed 'Prince of Speed', the English rider Phil Read rode for MV in the twilight of an illustrious career, which spanned some 20 years in the saddle. His first race came in 1956 on a BSA Gold Star. Later he switched to Norton machines and on one of these he shot to public attention by winning the Senior Manx GP in September 1960. Then in 1963 he joined the Scuderia Duke, but the team's four-cylinder Gilera machine did not suit him. The next move came in 1964 when he signed for Yamaha promptly winning his and the company's first World title on one of the 250 R656 twins. Then came three more titles before Yamaha pulled out at the end of 1968. After this Read rode specially prepared 'over-the-counter' Yamahas, culminating in another championship in 1971. Read signed for MV Agusta in early 1973, winning the 500 cc at his first attempt.

In 1974 Read became MV Agusta team leader as Ago had moved to Yamaha, and Gianfranco Bonera was signed as his replacement. At the Belgian GP that year Read wheeled out this 'winged' model, which was used in practice, but not raced. Read still won, however, for the 17th time in 17 years. Read went on to win the 500 cc World title to make it two in a row. This was to be MV's last championship.

An MV Agusta mechanic warms up the 500 MV four at a Brands Hatch meeting in 1974. A glorious era was coming to a close. Compare the paddock scene to today's: no motorhomes – but a nice Jensen Interceptor. This photograph captures all the atmosphere.

After finishing 2nd in the 500 cc series in 1975, the MV factory disbanded its official racing team of Phil Read and Gianfranco Bonera. Then Giacomo Agostini returned to the marque for 1976, fearing that Yamaha would withdraw its support of racing. Ago took over not only the latest 500 (illustrated), but also a new 350. Both were fours; the larger engine, in what was to be its final form, produced 98 bhp at 14,000 rpm. However, even though the speed was now up to 298 km/h (185 mph), it was still not fast or reliable enough to regain the title.

The final MV Agusta Grand Prix victory came in the last classic held in 1976: the 500 cc race at the Nürburgring, West Germany. Agostini kept the four-stroke ahead of the two-stroke pack to score – it was the machine's only finish in a Grand Prix that year. After a few 'flag-waving' exercises, such as appearances in England at Cadwell Park (Read) and Brands Hatch (Agostini), the plug was pulled on a racing effort that had lasted almost three decades, and had seen a record number of wins and championships at GP level.

A corner of the MV Agusta race shop at Perno in 1977. The dust is beginning to settle and the machines themselves are no longer awaiting transport to a race circuit. They are now only souvenirs – but what glorious souvenirs!

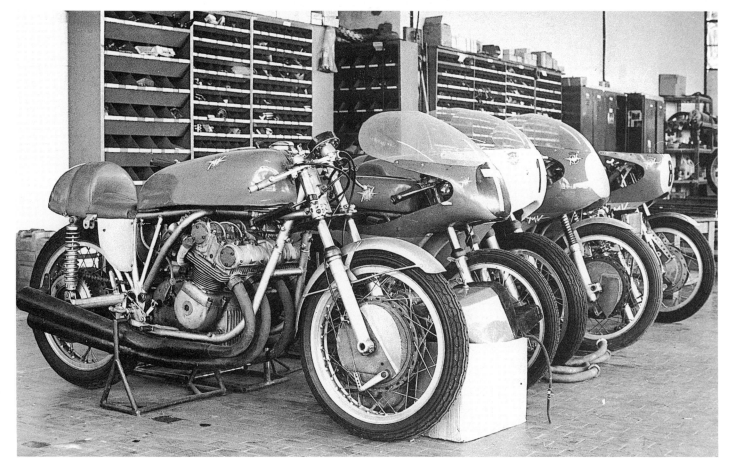

Parilla

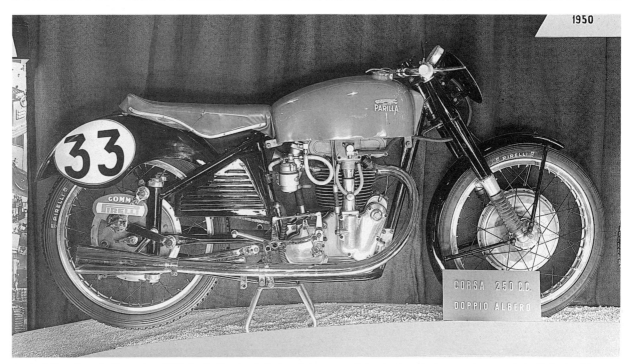

At the Milan Show in November 1950 the Parilla stand displayed its range of standard production roadsters and the limited edition works double-knocker 247 cc racer. Together with a 350 version, this machine was most successful not in Italy, but Germany, where they were specially tuned by the aptly surnamed Roland Schnell. With Hermann Gablenz, Schnell gained a string of victories and leader board positions throughout Germany and abroad during 1950 and 1951.

Designed in 1959-60, the 125 cc Parilla racing engine was the work of Ing. Bossaglia, who had taken his inspiration from East Germany's MZ and its designer, Walter Kaaden. Bore and stroke measurements were 55 x 52 mm, giving a capacity of 124 cc. The compression ratio was 14:1, and the power 23 bhp at 11,500 rpm. Drive was through a five-speed gearbox.

Parilla

The first motorcycle from Giovanni Parrilla (note the double 'r' surname) was a single overhead camshaft 250, which made its début as a racer in October 1947. Subsequently this was developed into a successful sports roadster which went on sale in 1950. The same year a double-knocker version appeared as the factory's answer to the all-conquering Moto Guzzi Albatros.

Both the single and double overhead camshaft engines for the Parilla (one 'r') range of motorcycles were designed by the prolific engineer Ing. Giuseppe Salmaggi (who also carried out work for Gilera, Rumi and FN among others).

Bottom left: Developed from the high camshaft roadster model, the 250 Parilla racer was sold both in Europe and North America during the early 1960s. One was also raced in the classic events by the Englishman Richard Morley, together with a 125 pushrod model, during 1965.

Bottom right: The disc-valve 125 Parilla stood idle for several years before Giovanni Parrilla took over its development as a private venture, after selling his share in the company in 1964. It was ridden with moderate success by an ex-Morini works rider, Giampiero Zubani, in the Italian Senior Championships in 1965.

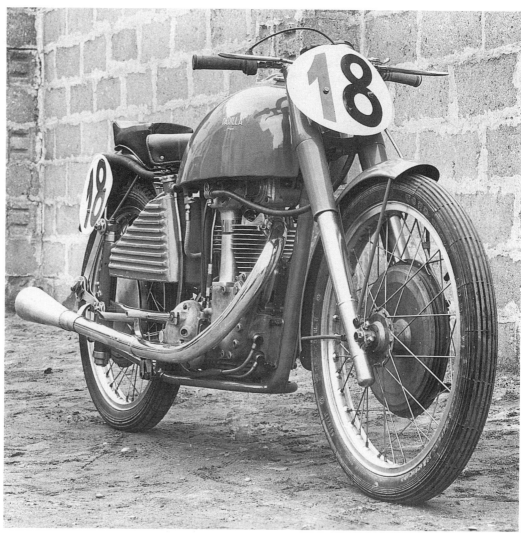

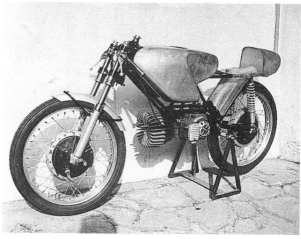

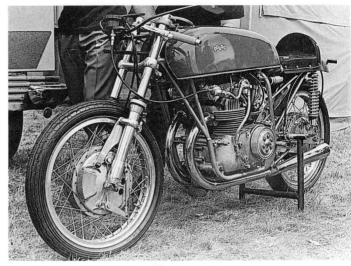

Paton

Above left: Giuseppe Pattoni was one of the key figures behind the scenes in the 125/250 cc Mondial World Championship double in 1957. After the company was disbanded at the end of the year Pattoni, with fellow engineer Lino Tonti, built a small number of 124 and 173 cc single-cylinder overhead camshaft racers based around Mondial components. One of the first customers for a Paton as the marque was called, was Mike Hailwood. In 1959 Tonti joined Bianchi and Pattoni designed a 250 twin. By 1964 a development of this was producing 34 bhp at 12,000 rpm with six speeds. Riders were Zubani and Pagani. *Above right:* In 1964 Alberto Pagani finished 3rd in the Lightweight TT. The following year a new machine was constructed by Pattoni in his small Milan workshop. Like the earlier examples, this 250 had a bore and stroke of 53 x 56 mm. Finished only days before the Dutch TT at the end of June, the bike was rushed to Assen where Pagani took it to 10th place. *Below left:* Canadian Mike Duff rode this 350 cc Paton twin at the Mallory Park 'Race of the Year' meeting on 26 September 1965. The machine, the first of its kind, was built by Giuseppe Pattoni for the Rhodesian Colin Lyster seen here with Duff. The double overhead camshaft engine revved to 11,000 and gave 40 bhp. Duff took 2nd place in his heat and 9th in a very wet final. *Below right:* In 1967 the first 500 cc class Paton arrived. Developed from the earlier twins, this had a capacity of 470.66 cc (72 x 52.8 mm) and offered 52 bhp at 9600 rpm. It won the Senior Italian Championships that year in the hands of Angelo Bergamonti. In 1970 Pattoni enlarged the engine to 483.68 cc by increasing the bore size to 73.5 mm. He is shown here working on the bike at the Italian GP that year. The team was sponsored at the time by Bill Hannah, a Liverpool-based Scot. Known as the Hannah-Patons, the main riders were Billie Nelson and Fred Stevens.

COMPETIZIONE
125 C C

Moto Rumi

Above: The Rumi factory introduced this racing version of its 124.68 cc (42 x 45 mm) horizontal twin at the Milan Show in November 1953. The Competizione was built only in very small numbers at the company's Bergamo plant; being replaced in 1955 by the Junior model, which was an almost totally different machine. This has made the Competizione highly sought after by collectors and Rumi enthusiasts alike. Notable features of the model included the huge magneto, which sat atop the crankcases; the short, stubby megaphone exhausts; a fuel tank which encased the steering column; and a pair of leading link front forks.

Former Rumi works rider Gianni Zonca reliving his past aboard a 1955 Junior at Misano in June 1989. Together with Bruno Romano, Zonca was the most successful of the riders sponsored by the factory. He was particularly successful in the Italian Championship series, and in long-distance races such as the Moto Giro and the Milan-Taranto.

Italian *Classic* Gallery

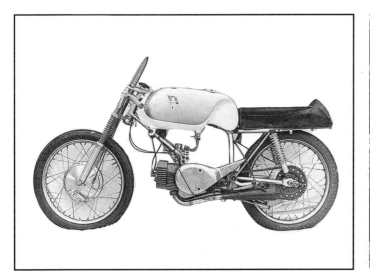

Top right: Rumi Special Gentleman. This was one of only seven built at the factory and is currently owned by Ricardo Crippa. The engine had essentially the same specification as the earlier Competizione.

Top left: From 1959, the Junior came with telescopic forks in place of the original Earles type and the styling was updated. One of the revised machines is seen here at the Silverstone Practice Day, 9 March 1960, ridden by Derek Wilson of New Malden, Surrey.

Above: The most successful British Rumi racer was the machine built and ridden by John Dixon, who is seen here leading Percy Tait, on a Ducati GP, at Oulton Park, September 1961. On this bike Dixon had a large number of wins and leader board placings to his credit throughout Britain in 1960 and 1961.

Vespa

On 9 February 1951 this very special 123 cc (42.9 x 44 mm) twin-cylinder Vespa streamliner, ridden by factory tester Mazzoncini, broke the 125 cc world speed record on the Rome-Ostia autostrada.

The engine was water-cooled but, unlike the similar Lambretta, it was not supercharged. Power output was 18 bhp at 9600 rpm. Running on methanol, the compression ratio was 11:1. There were two Dell'Orto carburettors and the machine weighed a total of 93 kg (205 lb). The ignition was produced by the parent Piaggio concern, as was the comprehensive fairing.

Villa

Although Francesco Villa no longer offered road racing motorcycles for sale, in 1974 he was asked by Claudio Lusuardi (later to sponsor an 80 cc racing project in the mid-1980s) to build a water-cooled 50 cc single. The result is shown here. It was of particularly neat design and, with its horizontal cylinder and low, lean lines, it was very much modelled on the West German Kreidlers, the class leaders. Maximum speed from the 20 bhp motor was around 177 km/h (110 mph).

Italian *Classic* Gallery

Francesco Villa was a successful works rider for several of the leading Italian manufacturers, including Ducati and Mondial. He was also responsible for developing machinery for Mondial and the Spanish Montesa concern. In 1968 Villa decided to branch out on his own. One of the first designs to carry his own name was this neat little 125 production racer. Its 123.15 cc (56 x 50 mm) disc valve, seven-speed power unit developed 28 bhp at 11,000 rpm. Riders in Italy and abroad found it both quick and reliable, especially in its later water-cooled form.

After the success of his single-cylinder 125 (and 250) racers, Francesco Villa turned his attention to a full GP bike. First he built a four-cylinder, narrow-angle V-four of 244 cc (43 x 42 mm). However the four was effectively banned by the new FIM international regulations and the Villa 250's only race was to be in the 1969 Italian GP. With the 250 four-cylinder unusable, Villa then used half the engine to create a narrow-angle 122 cc V-twin. With an output of 30 bhp, however, it was only slightly more powerful than the single – and obviously heavier. With the success of his company's offroad machinery, Villa reluctantly decided to concentrate his efforts on that sector and the 125 twin was abandoned.